I0631104

Charles Reginald Haines

Christianity and Islam in Spain, A.D. 756-1031 by Charles Reginald Haines

Charles Reginald Haines

Christianity and Islam in Spain, A.D. 756-1031 by Charles Reginald Haines

ISBN/EAN: 9783743357297

Manufactured in Europe, USA, Canada, Australia, Japa

Cover: Foto ©ninafisch / pixelio.de

Manufactured and distributed by brebook publishing software (www.brebook.com)

Charles Reginald Haines

Christianity and Islam in Spain, A.D. 756-1031 by Charles Reginald Haines

CHRISTIANITY AND ISLAM
IN SPAIN

A.D. 756-1031

BY

C. R. HAINES, M.A.

AUTHOR OF "ENGLAND AND THE OPIUM TRADE"; "EDUCATION AND MISSIONS";
"VERSIONS IN VERSE."

LONDON
KEGAN PAUL, TRENCH & CO., 1 PATERNOSTER SQUARE
1889

TABLE OF CONTENTS.

CHAPTER V.

CHAPTER VI.

CHAPTER VII.

CONTENTS.

APPENDICES.

APPENDIX A.

APPENDIX B.

CHAPTER I.

THE GOTHS IN SPAIN.

JUST about the time when the Romans withdrew from Britain, leaving so many of their possessions behind them, the Suevi, Alani, and Vandals, at the invitation of Gerontius, the Roman governor of Spain, burst into that province over the unguarded passes of the Pyrenees. Close on their steps followed the Visigoths; whose king, taking in marriage Placidia, the sister of Honorius, was acknowledged by the helpless emperor independent ruler of such parts of Southern Gaul and Spain as he could conquer and keep for himself. The effeminate and luxurious provincials offered practically no resistance to the fierce Teutons. No Arthur arose among them, as among the warlike Britons of our own island; no Viriathus even, as in the struggle for independence against the Roman Commonwealth. Mariana, the Spanish historian, asserts that they preferred the rule of the barbarians. However this may be, the various tribes that invaded the country found no serious opposition among the Spaniards: the only fighting was between themselves—for the spoil. Many years of warfare were necessary to decide this important question of supremacy. Fortunately for Spain, the Vandals, who seem to have been the fiercest horde and under the ablest leader, rapidly forced their way

---

[1] " Inter barbaros pauperem libertatem quam inter Romanos tributariam sollicitudinem sustinere."—Mariana, apud Dunham, vol. i.

A

southward, and, passing on to fresh conquests, crossed the Straits of Gibraltar in 429 : not, however, before they had utterly overthrown their rivals, the Suevi, on the river Baetis, and had left an abiding record of their brief stay in the name Andalusia.

For a time it seemed likely that the Suevi, in spite of their late crushing defeat, would subject to themselves the whole of Spain, but under Theodoric II. and Euric, the Visigoths definitely asserted their superiority. Under the latter king the Gothic domination in Spain may be said to have begun about ten years before the fall of the Western Empire. But the Goths were as yet by no means in possession of the whole of Spain. A large part of the south was held by imperialist troops ; for, though the Western Empire had been extinguished in 476, the Eastern emperor had succeeded by inheritance to all the outlying provinces, which had even nominally belonged to his rival in the West. Among these was some portion of Spain.

It was not till 570, the year in which Mohammed was born, that a king came to the Gothic throne strong enough to crush the Suevi and to reduce the imperialist garrisons in the South ; and it was not till 622, the very year of the Flight from Mecca, that a Gothic king, Swintila, finally drove out all the Emperor's troops, and became king in reality of all Spain.

Scarcely had this been well done, when we perceive the first indications of the advent of a far more terrible foe, the rumours of whose irresistible prowess had marched before them. The dread, which the Arabs aroused even in distant Spain as early as a century after the birth of Mohammed, may be appreciated from the despairing lines of Julian,[1] bishop of Toledo :—

---

[1] Migne's " Patrologie," vol. xcvi. p. 814.

" Hei mihi ! quam timeo, ne nos malus implicet error,
   Demur et infandis gentibus opprobrio !
Africa plena viris bellacibus arma minatur,
   Inque dies victrix gens Agarena furit."

Before giving an account of the Saracen invasion and its results, it will be well to take a brief retrospect of the condition of Christianity in Spain under the Gothic domination, and previous to the advent of the Moslems.

There can be no doubt that Christianity was brought very early into Spain by the preaching, as is supposed, of St Paul himself, who is said to have made a missionary journey through Andalusia, Valencia, and Aragon. On the other hand, there are no grounds whatever for supposing that James, the brother of John, ever set foot in Spain. The " invention " of his remains at Ira Flavia in the 9th century, together with the story framed to account for their presence in a remote corner of Spain so far from the scene of the Apostle's martyrdom, is a fable too childish to need refutation.

The honour of first hearing the Gospel message has been claimed (but, it seems, against probability) for Illiberis.[1] However that may be, the early establishment of Christianity in Spain is attested by Irenæus, who appeals to the Spanish Church as retaining the primitive doctrine.[2] The long roll of Spanish martyrs begins in the persecution of Domitian (95 A.D.) with the name of Eugenius, bishop of Toledo. In most of the succeeding persecutions Spain furnished her full quota of martyrs, but she suffered most under Diocletian (303). It was in this emperor's reign that nearly all the inhabitants of Cæsar Augusta were treacherously slaughtered on the sole ground of their being Christians ; thus earning for their native city from the Christian

---

[1] Florez, " España Sagrada," vol. iii. pp. 361 ff.
[2] Irenæus, Bk. I. ch. x. 2 (A.D. 186).

poet Prudentius,[1] the proud title of "patria sanctorum martyrum."

The persecution of Diocletian, though the fiercest, was at the same time the last, which afflicted the Church under the Roman Empire.   Diocletian indeed proclaimed that he had blotted out the very name of Christian and abolished their hateful superstition.   This even to the Romans must have seemed an empty boast, and the result of Diocletian's efforts only proved the truth of the old maxim—"the blood of martyrs is the seed of the Church."

The Spanish Christians about this time[2] held the first ecclesiastical council whose acts have come down to us. This Council of Illiberis, or Elvira, was composed of nineteen bishops and thirty-six presbyters, who passed eighty canons.

The imperial edict of toleration was issued in 313, and in 325 was held the first General Council of the Church under the presidency of the emperor, Constantine, himself an avowed Christian.   Within a quarter of a century of the time when Diocletian had boasted that he had extirpated the Christian name, it has been computed that nearly one half of the inhabitants of his empire were Christians.

The toleration, so long clamoured for, so lately conceded, was in 341 put an end to by the Christians themselves, and Pagan sacrifices were prohibited.   So inconsistent is the conduct of a church militant and a church triumphant! In 388, after a brief eclipse under Julian, Christianity was formally declared by the Senate to be the established religion of the Roman Empire.

But the security, or rather predominance, thus suddenly acquired by the church, resting as it did in part upon royal

---

[1] 348-402 A.D.

[2] The date is doubtful. Blunt, "Early Christianity," p. 209, places it between 314 and 325, though in a hesitating manner. Other dates given are 300 and 305.

favour and court intrigue, did not tend to the spiritual advancement of Christianity. Almost coincident with the Edict of Milan was the appearance of Arianism, which, after dividing the Church against itself for upwards of half-a-century, and almost succeeding at one time in imposing itself on the whole Church,[1] finally under the missionary zeal of Ulphilas found a new life among the barbarian nations that were pressing in upon all the northern boundaries of the Empire, ready, like eagles, to swoop down and feast upon her mighty carcase.

Most of these barbaric hordes, like the Goths and the Vandals, adopted the semi-Arian Christianity first preached to them by Ulphilas towards the close of the fourth century. Consequently the nations that forced their way into Southern Gaul, and over the Pyrenees into Spain, were, nominally at least, Christians of the Arian persuasion. The extreme importance to Spain of the fact of their being Christians at all will be readily apprehended by contrasting the fate of the Spanish provincials with that which befell the Christian and Romanized Britons at the hands of our own Saxon forefathers only half-a-century later.

Meanwhile the Church in Spain, like the Church elsewhere, freed from the quickening and purifying influences of persecution, had lost much of its ancient fervour. Gladiatorial shows and lascivious dances on the stage began to be tolerated even by Christians, though they were denounced by the more devout as incompatible with the profession of the Christian faith.

Spain also furnishes us with the first melancholy spectacle of Christian blood shed by Christian hands. Priscillian, bishop of Avila, was led into error by his intercourse with an Egyptian gnostic. What his error exactly was is not very clear, but it seems to have comprised some of the

[1] At the Council of Rimini in 360. "Ingemuit totus orbis," says Jerome, "et Arianum se esse miratus est."

erroneous doctrines attributed to Manes and Sabellius.   In 380, the new heresy, with which two other bishops besides Priscillian became infected, was condemned at a council held at Saragoza, and by another held five years later at Bordeaux.   Priscillian himself and six other persons were executed with tortures at the instigation of Ithacius,[1] bishop of Sossuba, and Idacius, bishop of Merida, in spite of the protests of Martin of Tours and others.   The heresy itself, however, was not thus stamped out, and continued in Spain until long after the Gothic conquest.

There is some reason for supposing that at the time of the Gothic invasion Spain was still in great part Pagan, and that it continued to be so during the whole period of Gothic domination.[2]   Some Pagans undoubtedly lingered on even as late as the end of the sixth century,[3] but that there were any large numbers of them as late as the eighth century is improbable.

Dr Dunham, who has given a clear and concise account of the Gothic government in Spain, calls it the "most accursed that ever existed in Europe."[4]   This is too sweeping a statement, though it must be allowed that the haughty exclusiveness of the Gothic nobles rendered their yoke peculiarly galling, while the position of their slaves was wretched beyond all example.   However, it is not to their civil administration that we wish now to draw attention, but rather to the relations of Church and State under a Gothic administration which was at first Arian and subsequently orthodox.

The Government, which began with being of a thoroughly

---

[1] See Milman, "Latin Christianity," vol. iii. p. 60.

[2] Dozy, ii. 44, quotes in support of this the second canon of the Sixteenth Council of Toledo.

[3] Mason, a bishop of Merida, was said to have baptized a Pagan as late as this.

[4] Dunham's "Hist. of Spain," vol. i. p. 210.

military character, gradually tended to become a theocracy—
a result due in great measure to the institution of national
councils, which were called by the king, and attended by
all the chief ecclesiastics of the realm. Many of the nobles
and high dignitaries of the State also took part in these
assemblies, though they might not vote on purely ecclesiastical matters. These councils, of which there were
nineteen in all (seventeen held at Toledo, the Gothic capital,
and two elsewhere), gradually assumed the power of ratifying
the election of the king, and of dictating his religious
policy. Thus by the Sixth Council of Toledo (canon
three) it was enacted that all kings should swear "not to
suffer the exercise of any other religion than the Catholic,
and to vigorously enforce the law against all dissentients,
especially against that accursed people the Jews." The
fact of the monarchy becoming elective[1] no doubt contributed a good deal to throwing the power into the hands
of the clergy.

Dr Dunham remarks that these councils tended to make
the bishops subservient to the court, but surely the evidence
points the other way. On the whole it was the king that
lost power, though no doubt as a compensation he gained
somewhat more authority over Church matters. He could,
for instance, issue temporary regulations with regard to
Church discipline. Witiza, one of the last of the Gothic
kings, seems even to have authorized, or at least encouraged, the marriage of his clergy.[2] The king could
preside in cases of appeal in purely ecclesiastical affairs ;
and we know that Recared I. (587-601) and Sisebert
(612-621) did in fact exercise this right. He also gained

[1] In 531 A.D.

[2] Monk of Silo, sec. 14, who follows Sebastian of Salamanca ;
Robertson, iii. 6. We learn from the "Chron. Sil," sec. 27, that
Fruela (757-768) forbade the marriage of clergy. But these accounts
of Witiza's reign are all open to suspicion.

the power of nominating and translating bishops; but it is not clear when this privilege was first conceded to the king.[1] The Fourth Council of Toledo (633) enacted that a bishop should be elected by the clergy and people of his city, and that his election should be approved by the metropolitan and synod of his province : while the Twelfth Council, held forty-eight years later, evidently recognizes the validity of their appointment by royal warrant alone. Some have referred this innovation back to the despotic rule of Theodoric the Ostrogoth, at the beginning of the sixth century; others to the sudden accumulation of vacant sees on the fall of Arianism in Spain. Another important power possessed by the kings was that of convoking these national councils, and confirming their acts.

The sudden surrender of their Arianism by the Gothic king and nobles is a noticeable phenomenon. All the barbarian races that invaded Spain at the beginning of the fifth century were inoculated with the Arian heresy. Of these the Vandals carried their Arianism, which proved to be of a very persecuting type, into Africa. The Suevi, into which nation the Alani, under the pressure of a common enemy, had soon been absorbed, gave up their Arianism for the orthodox faith about 560. The Visigoths, however, remained Arians until a somewhat later period—until 589 namely, when Recared I., the son of Leovigild, held a national council and solemnly abjured the creed of his forefathers, his example being followed by many of his nobles and bishops.

The Visigoths, while they remained Arian, were on the whole remarkably tolerant [2] towards both Jews and

---

[1] Robertson, "Hist. of Christian Church," vol. iii. p. 183.

[2] Lecky, "Rise of Rationalism," vol. i. p. 14, note, says that the Arian Goths were intolerant ; but there seem to be insufficient grounds for the assertion.

Catholics, though we have instances to the contrary in the cases of Euric and Leovigild, who are said to have persecuted the orthodox party. The latter king, indeed, who was naturally of a mild and forgiving temper, was forced into harsh measures by the unfilial and traitorous conduct of his son Ermenegild. If the latter had been content to avow his conversion to orthodoxy without entering into a treasonable rebellion in concert with the Suevi and Imperialists against his too indulgent father, there is every reason to think that Leovigild would have taken no measures against him. Even after a second rebellion the king offered to spare his son's life—which was forfeit to the State—on condition that he renounced his newly-adopted creed, and returned to the Arian fold. His reason—a very intelligible one—no doubt was that he might put an end to the risk of a third rebellion by separating his son effectually from the intriguing party of Catholics. To call Ermenegild a martyr because he was put to death under such circumstances is surely an abuse of words.

With the fall of Arianism came a large accession of bigotry to the Spanish Church, as is sufficiently shewn by the canon above quoted from the Sixth Council of Toledo. A subsequent law was even passed forbidding anyone under pain of confiscation of his property and perpetual imprisonment, to call in question the Holy Catholic and Apostolic Church ; the Evangelical Institutions; the definitions of the Fathers; the decrees of the Church ; and the Sacraments. In the spirit of these enactments, severe measures were taken against the Jews, of whom there were great numbers in Spain. Sisebert (612-621) seems to have been the first systematic persecutor, whose zeal, as even Isidore confesses, was " not according to knowledge." [1]   A cruel

---

[1] Apud Florez, "Esp. Sagr.," vol. vi. p. 502, quoted by Southey, Roderic, p. 255, n.   "Sisebertus, qui in initio regni Judaeos ad fidem Christianam permovens, aemulationem quidem habuit, sed non

choice was given the Jews between baptism on the one hand, and scourging and destitution on the other. When this proved unavailing, more stringent edicts were enforced against them. Those who under the pressure of persecution consented to be baptised, were forced to swear by the most solemn of oaths that they had in very truth renounced their Jewish faith and abhorred its rites. Those who still refused to conform were subjected to every indignity and outrage. They were obliged to have Christian servants, and to observe Sunday and Easter. They were denied the *ius connubii* and the *ius honorum*. Their testimony was invalid in law courts, unless a Christian vouched for their character. Some who still held out were even driven into exile. But this punishment could not have been systematically carried out, for the Saracen invasion found great numbers of Jews still in Spain. As Dozy[1] well says of the persecutors—"On le voulut bien, mais on ne le pouvait pas."

Naturally enough, under these circumstances the Jews of Spain turned their eyes to their co-religionists in Africa; but, the secret negotiations between them being discovered, the persecution blazed out afresh, and the Seventeenth Council of Toledo[2] decreed that relapsed Jews should be sold as slaves; that their children should be forcibly taken from them; and that they should not be allowed to marry among themselves.[3]

These odious decrees against the Jews must be attributed to the dominant influence of the clergy, who requited the help they thus received from the secular arm by wielding the powers of anathema and excommunication against the

secundum scientiam : potestate enim compulit, quos provocare fidei ratione oportuit. Sed, sicut est scriptum, sive per occasionem sive per veritatem Christus annunciatur, in hoc gaudeo et gaudebo."

[1] "History of Mussulmans in Spain," vol. ii. p. 26.

[2] Canon 8, de damnatione Judaeorum.

[3] For the further history of the Jews in Spain, see Appendix A.

political enemies of the king.[1] Moreover the cordial relations which subsisted between the Church and the State, animated as they were by a strong spirit of independence, enabled the Spanish kings to resist the dangerous encroachments of the Papal power, a subject which has been more fully treated in an Appendix.[2]

———o———

CHAPTER II.

THE SARACENS IN SPAIN.

THE Gothic domination lasted 300 years, and in that comparatively short period we are asked by some writers to believe that the invaders quite lost their national characteristics, and became, like the Spaniards, luxurious and effeminate.[3] Their haughty exclusiveness, and the fact of their being Arians, may no doubt have tended to keep them for a time separate from, and superior to, the subject population, whom they despised as slaves, and hated as heretics. But when the religious barrier was removed, the social one soon followed, and so completely did the conquerors lose their ascendency, that they even surrendered their own Teutonic tongue for the corrupt Latin of their subjects.

But the Goths had certainly not become so degenerate as is generally supposed. Their Saracen foes did not thus

[1] The councils are full of denunciations aimed at the rebels against the king's authority. By the Fourth Council (633) the deposed Swintila was excommunicated.

[2] Appendix B.

[3] Cardonne's " History of Spain," vol. i. p. 62. " Bien différens des leurs ancêtres étoient alors énervés par les plaisirs, la douceur du climat ; le luxe et les richesses avoient amolli leur courage et corrompu les moeurs." Cp. Dunham, vol. i. 157.

undervalue them.   Musa ibn Nosseyr, the organiser of the
expedition into Spain, and the first governor of that country
under Arab rule, when asked by the Khalif Suleiman for
his opinion of the Goths, answered that "they were lords
living in luxury and abundance, but champions who did
not turn their backs to the enemy."[1]   There can be no
doubt that this praise was well deserved.   Nor is the
comparative ease with which the country was overrun, any
proof to the contrary.   For that must be attributed to
wholesale treachery from one end of the country to the
other.   But for this the Gothic rulers had only themselves
to blame.   Their treatment of the Jews and of their slaves
made the defection of these two classes of their subjects
inevitable.

The old Spanish chroniclers represent the fall of the
Gothic kingdom as the direct vengeance of Heaven for
the sins of successive kings;[2] but on the heads of the
clergy, even more than of the king, rests the guilt of their
iniquitous and suicidal policy towards the Arians[3] and the
Jews.   The treachery of Julian,[4] whatever its cause, opened
a way for the Arabs into the country by betraying into
their hands Ceuta, the key of the Straits.   Success in their
first serious battle was secured to them by the opportune
desertion from the enemy's ranks of the disaffected political
party under the sons of the late king Witiza,[5] and an

---

[1] Al Makkari, vol. i. p. 297.   (De Gayangos' translation).

[2] "Chron. Sil.," sec. 17, "recesserat ab Hispania manus Domini
ob inveteratam regum malitiam."   See above, p. 7, note 2.

[3] Arianism lingered on till the middle of the eighth century at least,
since Rodrigo of Toledo, iii., sec. 3, says of Alfonso I., that he "extir-
pavit haeresin Arianam."

[4] For Julian, or, more correctly, Ilyan, see De Gayangos' note to Al
Makkari, i. p. 537, etc.

[5] Called Ghittishah by the Arabs.   For the Witizan party see
"Sebast. Salan," sec. 7; "Chron. Sil.," sec. 15.   The daughter of
Witiza married a noble Arab.   The descendants of the King, under
the name Witizani, were known in Spain till the end of the eighth

archbishop Oppas, who afterwards apostatized; while the rapid subjugation of the whole country was aided and assured by the hosts of ill-used slaves who flocked to the Saracen standards, and by the Jews[1] who hailed the Arabs as fellow-Shemites and deliverers from the hated yoke of the uncircumcised Goths.

Yet in spite of all these disadvantages the Goths made a brave stand—as brave, indeed, as our Saxon forefathers against the Normans. The first decisive battle in the South[2] lasted, as some writers have declared, six whole days, and the Arabs were at one time on the point of being driven into the sea. This is apparent from Tarik's address to his soldiers in the heat of battle : " Moslems, conquerors of Africa, whither would you fly? The sea is behind you, and the foe in front. There is no help for you save in your own right hands[3] and the favour of God." Nor must we lay any stress on the disparity of forces on either side, amounting to five to one, for a large proportion of Roderic's army was disaffected. It is probable that only the Goths made a determined stand ; and even after such a crushing defeat as they received at Guadalete, and after the loss of their king, the Gothic nobles still offered a stubborn resistance in Merida, Cordova, and elsewhere.[4] One of

century at least. See Letter of Beatus and Etherius to Elipandus, sec. 61 : "Multi hodie ab ipso rege sumunt nomen *Witizani*, etiam pauperes." See also Al Makkari, ii. 14.

[1] The Jews garrisoned the taken towns (Al Makkari, i. pp. 280, 282, and De Gayangos' note, p. 531). Even as late as 852 we find the Jews betraying Barcelona to the Moors, who slew nearly all the Christians.

[2] Generally called the battle of Guadalete (Wada Lek, see De Gayangos on Al Makk. i. pp. 524, 527), fought either near Xeres or Medina Sidonia.

[3] "Una salus victis nullam sperare salutem." See Al Makk. i. p. 271; Conde i. p. 57 (Bohn's Translation).

[4] We must not forget also that the mild and politic conduct of the Saracens towards the towns that surrendered, even after resistance, marvellously facilitated their conquest.

them, Theodomir, after defending himself manfully in
Murcia for some time, at last by his valour and address
contrived to secure for himself, and even to hand down
to his successor Athanagild, a semi-independent rule over
that part of Spain.

But the great proof that the Goths had not lost all their
ancient hardihood and nobleness, is afforded by the fact
that, when they had been driven into the mountains of
the North and West, they seem to have begun at once to
organize a fresh resistance against the invaders. The thirty[1]
wretched barbarians, whom the Arabs thought it unnecessary
to pursue into their native fastnesses, soon showed that
they had power to sting; and the handful of patriots, who
in the cave of Covadonga gathered round Pelayo, a scion
of the old Gothic line, soon swelled into an army, and the
army into a nation. Within six years of the death of
Roderic had begun that onward march of the new Spanish
monarchy, which, with the exception of a disastrous twenty-
five years at the close of the tenth century, was not destined
to retrograde, scarcely even to halt, until it had regained
every foot of ground that had once belonged to the Gothic
kings.

Let us turn for a moment to the antecedents of the Arab
invaders. History affords no parallel, whether from a
religious or political point of view, to the sudden rise of
Mohammedanism and the wonderful conquests which it
made. " The electric spark[2] had indeed fallen on what
seemed black unnoticeable sand, and lo the sand proved
explosive powder and blazed heaven-high from Delhi to
Granada!" Mohammed began his preaching in 609, and
confined himself to persuasion till 622, the year of the
Flight from Mecca. After this a change seems to have

[1] Al Makk., ii. 34. "What are thirty barbarians perched upon a
rock? They must inevitably die."

[2] Carlyle's " Hero Worship " ad finem.

come over his conduct, if not over his character, and the Prophet, foregoing the peaceful and more glorious mission of a Heaven-sent messenger, appealed to the human arbitrament of the sword : not with any very marked success, however, the victory of Bedr in 624 being counterbalanced by the defeat of Ohud in in the following year. In 631, Arabia being mostly pacified, the first expedition beyond its boundaries was undertaken under Mohammed's own leadership, but this abortive attempt gave no indications of the astonishing successes to be achieved in the near future. Mohammed himself died in the following year, yet, in spite of this and the consequent revolt of almost all Arabia, within two years Syria was overrun and Damascus taken. Persia, which had contended for centuries on equal terms with Rome, was overthrown in a single campaign. In 637 Jerusalem fell, and the sacred soil of Palestine passed under the yoke of the Saracens. Within three years Alexandria and the rich valley of the Nile were the prize of Amru and his army. The conquest of Egypt only formed the stepping-stone to the reduction of Africa, and the victorious Moslems did not pause in their career until they reached the Atlantic Ocean, and Akbah,[1] riding his horse into the sea, sighed for more worlds to conquer. We may be excused perhaps for thinking that it had been well for the inhabitants of the New World, if Fortune had delivered them into the hands of the generous Arabs rather than to the cruel soldiery of Cortes and Pizarro.

In 688, that is, in a little more than a generation from the death of Mohammed, the Moslems undertook the siege of Constantinople. Fortunately for the cause of civilisation and of Christendom, this long siege of several years proved unsuccessful, as well as a second attack in 717. But by the latter date the footing in Europe, which the

---

[1] Cardonne, i. p. 37 ; Gibbon, vi. 348, note.

valour of the Byzantines denied them, had already been
gained by the expedition into Spain under Tarik in 711.
The same year that witnessed the crossing of the Straits of
Gibraltar in the West saw also in the East the passage of
the Oxus by the eager warriors of Islam.

There seems to be some ground for supposing that the
Saracens had attacked Spain even before the time of Tarik.
As early as 648, or only one year after the invasion of
Africa, an expedition is said to have been made into that
country under Abdullah ibn Sa'd,[1] which resulted in the
temporary subjugation of the southern provinces. A
second inroad is mentioned by Abulfeda[2] as having taken
place in Othman's reign (644-656); while for an incursion
in the reign of Wamba (671-680) we have the authority of
the Spanish historians, Isidore of Beja and Sebastian of
Salamanca, the former of whom adds the fact that the
Saracens were invited in by Erviga, who afterwards succeeded Wamba on the throne—a story which seems likely
enough when read in the light of the subsequent treason
of Julian. These earlier attacks, however, seem to have
been mere raids, undertaken without an immediate view
to permanent conquest.

By way of retaliation, or with a commendable foresight,
the Goths sent help to Carthage when besieged by the
Arabs in 695; and, while Julian their general still remained
true to his allegiance, they beat off the Saracens from Ceuta.
But on the surrender of that fortress the Arabs were enabled
to send across the Straits a small reconnoitring detachment
of five hundred men under Tarif abu Zarah,[3] a Berber. This

---

[1] See De Gayangos' note on Al Makkari, i. p. 382.

[2] "Annales Moslemici," i. p. 262.

[3] The names of Tarif ibn Malik abu Zarah and Tarik ibn Zeyad have
been confused by all the careless writers on Spanish history—*e.g.*, Conde,
Dunham, Yonge, Southey, etc. ; but Gibbon, Freeman, etc., of course
do not fall into this error. For Tarif's names see De Gayangos, Al

took place in October 710; but the actual invasion did not occur till April 30, 711, when 12,000 men landed under Tarik ibn Zeyad. There seems to have been a preliminary engagement before the decisive one of Gaudalete (July 19th-26th)—the Gothic general in the former being stated variously to have been Theodomir,[1] Sancho,[2] or Edeco.[3]

It will not be necessary to pursue the history of the conquest in detail. It is enough to say that in three years almost all Spain and part of Southern Gaul were added to the Saracen empire. But the Arabs made the fatal mistake[4] of leaving a remnant of their enemies unconquered in the mountains of Asturia, and hardly had the wave of conquest swept over the country, than it began slowly but surely to recede. The year 733 witnessed the high-water mark of Arab extension in the West, and Christian Gaul was never afterwards seriously threatened with the calamity of a Mohammedan domination.

The period of forty-five years which elapsed between the conquest and the establishment of the Khalifate of Cordova was a period of disorder, almost amounting to anarchy, throughout Spain. This state of things was one eminently favourable to the growth and consolidation of the infant state which was arising among the mountains of the Northwest. In that corner of the land, which alone[5] was not polluted by the presence of Moslem masters, were gathered all those proud spirits who could not brook subjection and valued freedom above all earthly possessions.[6] Here all

Makk., i. pp. 517, 519; and for Tarik's see "Ibn Abd el Hakem," Jones' translation, note 10.

[1] Al Makk., i. 268 : Isidore : Conde, i. 55.

[2] Cardonne, i. 75.   [3] Dr Dunham.   [4] Al Makkari, ii. 34.

[5] According to Sebastian of Salamanca, the Moors had never been admitted into any town of Biscay before 870.

[6] Prescott, "Ferdinand and Isabella," seems to think that only the lower orders remained under the Moors. Yet in a note he mentions a remark of Zurita's to the contrary (page 3).

the various nationalities that had from time to time borne
rule in Spain,

" Punic and Roman Kelt and Goth and Greek," [1]

all the various classes, nobles, freemen, and slaves, were
gradually welded by the strong pressure of a common
calamity into one compact and homogeneous whole.[2]
Meanwhile what was the condition of those Christians
who preferred to live in their own homes, but under the
Moslem yoke ?   It must be confessed that they might have
fared much worse ; and the conciliatory policy pursued by
the Arabs no doubt contributed largely to the facility of the
conquest.   The first conqueror, Tarik ibn Zeyad, was a man
of remarkable generosity and clemency, and his conduct
fully justified the proud boast which he uttered when
arraigned on false charges before the Sultan Suleiman.[3]
'Ask the true believers," he said, " ask also the Christians,
what the conduct of Tarik has been in Africa and in Spain.
Let them say if they have ever found him cowardly, covetous,
or cruel."

The terms granted to such towns as surrendered generally
contained the following provisions : that the citizens should
give up all their horses and arms ; that they might, if they
chose, depart, leaving their property ; that those who remained should, on payment of a small tribute, be permitted

[1] Southey, " Roderick," Canto IV.

[2] Thierry, " Dix Ans d'Études Historiques," p. 346.   " Reserrés dans
ce coin de terre, devenu pour eux toute la patrie, Goths et Romains,
vainqueurs et vaincus, étrangers et indigènes, maîtres et esclaves, tous
unis dans le même malheur . . . furent égaux dans cet exil."   Yet
there were revolts in every reign.   Fruela I. (757-768), revolt of
Biscay and Galicia : Aurelio (768-774), revolt of slaves and freedmen,
see " Chron. Albeld.," vi. sec. 4, and Rodrigo, iii. c. 5, in pristinam
servitutem redacti sunt : Silo (774-783), Galician revolt : also revolts
in reigns of Alfonso I., Ramiro I.   See Prescott, " Ferd. and Isab.,"
p. 4.

[3] Or his predecessor, Welid, for the point is not determined.

to follow their own religion, for which purposes certain churches were to be left standing; that they should have their own judges, and enjoy (within limits) their own laws. In some cases the riches of the churches were also surrendered, as at Merida,[1] and hostages given. But conditions even better than these were obtained from Abdulaziz, son of Musa, by Theodomir in Murcia. The original document has been preserved by the Arab historians, and is well worthy of transcription:

"In the name of God the Clement and Merciful! Abdulaziz and Tadmir make this treaty of peace—may God confirm and protect it! Tadmir shall retain the command over his own people, but over no other people among those of his faith. There shall be no wars between his subjects and those of the Arabs, nor shall the children or women of his people be led captive. They shall not be disturbed in the exercise of their religion: their churches shall not be burnt, nor shall any services be demanded from them, or obligations be laid upon them—those expressed in this treaty alone excepted. . . . Tadmir shall not receive our enemies, nor fail in fidelity to us, and he shall not conceal whatever hostile purposes he may know to exist against us. His nobles and himself shall pay a tribute of a dinar [2] each year, with four measures of wheat and four of barley; of mead, vinegar, honey, and oil each four measures. All the vassals of Tadmir, and every man subject to tax, shall pay the half of these imposts." [3]

These favourable terms were due in part to the address of Theodomir,[4] and partly perhaps to Abdulaziz's own

---

[1] Conde i. p. 69. This was perhaps due to Musa's notorious avarice.

[2] Somewhat less than ten shillings.

[3] Al Makkari, i. 281 : Conde, i. p. 76.

[4] Isidore, sec, 38, says of him : " Fuit scripturarum amator, eloquentia mirificus, in proeliis expeditus, qui et apud Amir Almumenin prudentior inter ceteros inventus, utiliter est honoratus."

partiality for the Christians, which was also manifested in his marriage with Egilona, the widow of King Roderic, and the deference which he paid to her. This predilection for the Christians brought the son of Musa into ill favour with the Arabs, and he was assassinated in 716.[1]

On the whole it may be said that the Saracen conquest was accomplished with wonderfully little bloodshed, and with few or none of those atrocities which generally characterize the subjugation of a whole people by men of an alien race and an alien creed. It cannot, however, be denied that the only contemporary Christian chronicler is at variance on this point with all the Arab accounts.

" Who," says Isidore of Beja, " can describe such horrors ! If every limb in my body became a tongue, even then would human nature fail in depicting this wholesale ruin of Spain, all its countless and immeasurable woes. But that the reader may hear in brief the whole story of sorrow—not to speak of all the disastrous ills which in innumerable ages past from Adam even till now in various states and regions of the earth a cruel and foul foe has caused to a fair world —whatever Troy in Homer's tale endured, whatever Jerusalem suffered that the prophets' words might come to pass, whatever Babylon underwent that the Scripture might be fulfilled—all this, and more, has Spain experienced—Spain once full of delights, but now of misery, once so exalted in glory, but now brought low in shame and dishonour." [2]

This is evidently mere rhapsody, of the same character

---

[1] Al Makkari, ii. p. 30. He was even accused of entering into treasonable correspondence with the Christians of Galicia ; of forming a project for the massacre of Moslems ; of being himself a Christian, etc.

[2] Cp. also Isidore, sec 36. Dunham, ii. p. 121, note, curiously remarks : " Both Isidore and Roderic may exaggerate, but the exaggeration proves the fact."

as the ravings of the British monk Gildas, though far less justified as it seems by the actual facts. Rodrigo of Toledo, following Isidore after an interval of 500 years, improves upon him by entering into details, which being in many particulars demonstrably false, may in others be reasonably looked upon with suspicion as exaggerated, if not entirely imaginary. His words are : Children are dashed on the ground, young men beheaded, their fathers fall in battle, the old men are massacred, the women reserved for greater misfortune ; every cathedral burnt or destroyed, the national substance plundered, oaths and treaties uniformly broken.[1]

To appreciate the mildness and generosity of the Arabs, we need only compare their conquest of Spain with the conquest of England by the Saxons, the Danes, and even by the Christian Normans. The comparison will be all in favour of the Arabs. It is not impossible that, if the invaders had been Franks instead of Moors, the country would have suffered even more, as we can see from the actual results effected by the invasion of Charles the Great in 777. Placed as they were between the devil and the deep sea, the Spaniards would perhaps have preferred (had the choice been theirs) to be subject to the Saracens rather than to the Franks.[2]

To the down-trodden slaves, who were very numerous all through Spain, the Moslems came in the character of deliverers. A slave had only to pronounce the simple formula: "There is no God but God, and Mohammed is his Prophet": and he was immediately free. To the Jews the Moslems brought toleration, nay, even influence and power. In fact, since the fall of Jerusalem in 588 B.C. the

---

[1] Dunham, ii. p. 121, note.
[2] Dozy, ii. p. 41, note, quotes Ermold Nigel on Barcelona :

"Urbs erat interea Francorum inhospita turmis,
Maurorum votis adsociata magis."

Jews had never enjoyed such independence and influence as in Spain during the domination of the Arabs. Their genius being thus allowed free scope, they disputed the supremacy in literature and the arts with the Arabs themselves.

Many of the earlier governors of Spain were harsh and even cruel in their administration, but it was to Moslems and Christians alike.[1] Some indeed increased the tribute laid upon the Christians; but it must be remembered that this tribute[2] was in the first instance very light, and therefore an increase was not felt severely as an oppression. Moreover, there were not wanting some rulers who upheld the cause of the Christians against illegal exactions. Among these was Abdurrahman al Ghafcki (May-Aug. 721, and 731-732), of whom an Arab writer says:[3] "He did equal justice to Moslem and Christian . . . he restored to the Christians such churches as had been taken from them in contravention of the stipulated treaties; but on the other hand he caused all those to be demolished, which had been erected by the connivance of interested governors." Similarly of his successor Anbasah ibn Sohaym Alkelbi (721-726), we find it recorded[4] that "he rendered equal justice to every man, making no distinction between Mussulman and Christian, or between Christian and Jew." Anbasah was followed by Yahya ibn Salmah (March-Sept. 726), who is described as injudiciously severe, and dreaded for his extreme rigour by Moslems as well as Christians.[5] Isidore says that he made the Arabs give back to the Christians

---

[1] *E.g.*, Alhorr ibn Abdurrahman (717-719); see Isidore, sec. 44, and Conde, i. 94: "He oppressed all alike, the Christians, those who had newly embraced Islam, and the oldest of the Moslemah families."

[2] Merely a small poll-tax (jizyah) at first.

[3] Conde, i. 105.

[4] Conde, i. p. 99. Isidore, however, sec. 52, says: "Vectigalia Christianis duplicata exagitat."

[5] Conde, i. 102.

the property unlawfully taken from them.[1]   Similar praise
is awarded to Okbah ibn ulhejaj Asseluli (734-740).[2]   Yet
though many of the Ameers of Spain were just and upright
men, no permanent policy could be carried out with
regard to the relations between Moslems and Christians,
while the Ameers were so constantly changing, being sometimes elected by the army, but oftener appointed by the
Khalif, or by his lieutenant, the governor of Africa for the
time being.   This perpetual shifting of rulers would in
itself have been fatal to the settlement of the country. had
it not been brought to an end by the election of Abdurrahman ibn Muawiyah as the Khalif of Spain, and the establishment of his dynasty on the throne, in May 756.   But
even after this important step was taken, the causes which
threatened to make anarchy perpetual, were still at work
in Spain.   Chief among these were the feuds of the Arab
tribes, and the jealousy between Berbers and Arabs.

Most of the first conquerors of the country were Berbers,
while such Arabs as came in with them belonged mostly to
the Maadite or Beladi faction.[3]   The Berbers, besides being
looked down upon as new converts, were also regarded as
Nonconformists [4] by the pure Arabs, and consequently a
quarrel was not long in breaking out between the two parties.

As early as 718 the Berbers in Aragon and Catalonia

[1] Isidore, sec. 54.   Terribilis potestator fere triennio crudelis
exaestuat, atque acri ingenio Hispaniae Sarracenos et Mauros pro
pacificis rebus olim ablatis exagitat, atque Christianis plura restaurat.

[2] Conde, i. 114, 115.

[3] The two chief branches of Arabs were (1) Descendants of Modhar,
son of Negus, son of Maad, son of Adnan.   To this clan belonged the
Mecca and Medina Arabs, and the Umeyyade family.   They were
also called Kaysites, Febrites, and Beladi Arabs. (2) Descendants
of Kahtan (Joktan), among whom were reckoned the Kelbites and the
Yemenites.   These were most numerous in Andalus; see Al Makkari,
ii. 24.

[4] Dozy, iii. 124.   See Al Makk., ii. 409, De Gayangos' note.
Though nominally Moslem, they still kept their Jewish or Pagan rites.

rose against the Arabs under a Jew named Khaulan, who
was put to death the following year. In 726 they revolted
again, crying that they who had conquered the country
alone had claims to the spoil.[1] This formidable rising was
only put down by the Arabs making common cause against
it. But the continual disturbances in Africa kept alive the
flame of discontent in Spain, and the great Berber rebellion
against the Arab yoke in Africa was a signal for a similar
determined attempt in Spain.[2] The reinforcements which
the Khalif, Yezid ibn Abdulmalik, sent to Africa under
Kolthum ibn Iyadh were defeated by the Berbers under a
chief named Meysarah, and shut up in Ceuta.

Meanwhile in Spain, Abdalmalik ibn Kattan[3] Alfehri
taking up the cause of the Berbers, procured the deposition
of Okbah ibn ulhejaj in his own favour, but, this done, broke
with his new allies. He was then compelled to ask the
help of the Syrian Arabs, who were cooped up in Ceuta,
though previously he had turned a deaf ear to their
entreaties that they might cross over into Spain.

The Syrians gladly accepted this invitation, and under
Balj ibn Besher, nephew of Kolthum, crossed the Straits,
readily promising at the same time to return to Africa when
the Spanish Berbers were overcome. This desirable end
accomplished, however, they refused to keep to their agreement, and Abdalmalik soon found himself driven to seek
anew the alliance of the Berbers and also of the Andalusian
Arabs against his late allies.[4] But the latter proved too

---

[1] See De Gayangos, Al Makk. ii. 410, note. He quotes Borbon's
"Karta," xiv. *sq.* Stanley Lane-Poole, "Moors in Spain," p. 55,
says, Monousa, who married the daughter of Eudes, was a leader of
the Berbers. Conde, i. 106, says, Othman abi Neza was the leader, but
Othman ibn abi Nesah was Ameer of Spain in 728.

[2] Al Makkari, ii. 40.   [3] Cardonne, i. p. 135.

[4] The Syrian Arabs seem to have borne a bad character away from
home. The Sultan Muawiyah warned his son that they altered for the
worse when abroad. See Ockley's "Saracens."

strong for the Ameer, who was defeated and killed by the Yemenite followers of Balj.

These feuds of Yemenites against Modharites, complicated by the accession of Berbers now to one side, now to the other, continued without intermission till the first Khalif of Cordova, Abdurrahman ibn Muawiyah, established his power all over Spain.

The successor of Balj and Thaleba ibn Salamah did indeed try to break up the Syrian faction by separating them. He placed those of Damascus in Elvira; of Emesa in Seville; of Kenesrin in Jaen; of Alurdan[1] in Malaga and Regio; of Palestine in Sidonia or Xeres; of Egypt in Murcia; of Wasit in Cabra; and they thus became merged into the body of Andalusian Arabs.

These Berber wars had an important influence on the future of Spain; for, since the Berbers had settled on all the Northern and Western marches, when they were decimated by civil war, and many of the survivors compelled to return to Africa,[2] owing to the famine which afflicted the country from 750 to 755, the frontiers of the Arab dominion were left practically denuded of defenders,[3] and the Christians at once advanced their boundaries to the Douro, leaving however a strip of desert land as a barrier between them and the Moslems. This debateable land they did not occupy till fifty years later.[4]

---

[1] *I.e.*, Jordan. See Al Makkari, i. 356, De Gayangos' note.
[2] Dozy, iii. 24.   [3] Al Makkari, ii. 69.
[4] When they built a series of fortresses as Zamora, Simancas, San Estevan.

———*o*———

CHAPTER III.

THE MARTYRDOMS AT CORDOVA.

ABDURRAHMAN IBN MUAWIYAH landed in Spain with 750 Berber horsemen in May 756. The Khalifate of Cordova may be said to begin with this date, though it was many years before the new sultan had settled his power on a firm basis, or was recognised as ruler by the whole of Moslem Spain.

During the forty-five years of civil warfare which intervened between the invasion of Tarik and the landing of Abdurrahman, we have very little knowledge of what the Christians were doing. The Arab historians are too busy recounting the feuds of their own tribes to pay any particular attention to the subject Christians. But we may gather that the latter were, on the whole, fairly content with their new servitude.[1] The Moslems were not very anxious to proselytize, as the conversion of the Spaniards meant a serious diminution of the tribute.[2] Those Christians who did apostatize—and we may believe that they were chiefly slaves—at once took up a position of legal, though not social, equality with the other Moslems. It is no wonder that the slaves became Mohammedans, for, apart from their hatred for their masters, and the obvious temporal advantage of embracing Islam, the majority of them knew nothing at all about Christianity.[3] The ranks of the

---

[1] This was not so when the fierce Almoravides and fiercer Almohades overran Spain in the eleventh and twelfth centuries. See Freeman's "Saracens," p. 168.

[2] As happened in Egypt under Amru. See Cardonne, i. p. 168, and Gibbon, vi. p. 370.

[3] Dozy, ii. 45, quotes a passage from Pedraça, "Histor. Eccles. of Granada" (1638), in which the author points out that even in his day the "old Christians" of Central Spain were so wholly ignorant of all Chris-

converts were recruited from time to time by those who went over to Islam to avoid paying the poll-tax, or even to escape the payment of some penalty inflicted by the Christian courts.[1] One thing is noticeable. In the early years of the conquest there was none of that bitterness displayed between the adherents of the rival creeds, to which we are so accustomed in later times. Isidore of Beja, the only contemporary Christian authority, though he rhapsodizes about the devastations committed by the conquerors, and complains of enormous tributes exacted, yet speaks more fairly about the Moslems[2] than any other Spanish writer before the fourteenth century. "If he hates the conquerors," says Dozy,[3] "he hates them rather as men of another race than of another creed;" and the marriage of Abdulaziz and Egilona awakens in his mind no sentiment of horror.

On the whole the condition of the mass of the people, Christian or renegade, was certainly preferable to their state before the conquest.[4] Those serfs who remained Christian, if they worked on State lands, payed one-third of the produce to the State; if on private lands, four-fifths to their Arab owners.[5] The free Christians retained their goods, and could even alienate their lands. They paid a graduated tax varying from thirteen pounds to three guineas.[6] In all probability the Christians under Moslem rule were not worse off than their coreligionists in Galicia and Leon. A signal proof of this is afforded by the fact that, in spite of the distracted state of the country, which would seem to hold out a great hope of success, we hear of no attempts at revolt on the part of the subjected Christians in the eighth century,

tian doctrines that they might be expected to renounce Christianity with the utmost ease if again subjected to the Moors.

[1] Samson, "Apolog.," ii. cc. 3, 5.

[2] Speaking of Omar, the second Khalif of that name, Isidore, sec. 46, says, "Tanta ei sanctimonia ascribitur quanta nulli unquam ex Arabum gente." [3] Dozy, ii. p. 42.

[4] See especially Conde, Pref. p. vi. [5] Dozy, ii. 39. [6] Dozy, ii. 40.

except at Beja, where the Christians seem to have been led away by the ambition of an Arab chief.[1]   They were even somewhat indifferent to the cause of their coreligionists in the North, and the attempts which Pelayo and his successors made to induce them to rise in concert with their brethren met with but scant success.[2]

There can be no doubt, however, that the good understanding, which at first existed between the Moslems and their Christian subjects, gradually gave place to a very different state of things, owing in no small degree to the free Christians in the North, whose presence on their borders was a continual menace to the Moslem dominion, and a perpetual incentive to the subject Christians to rise and assert their freedom.

Our purpose now is to trace out, so far as the scanty indications scattered in the writers of the time will allow, the relations that existed between the two religions during the 275 years of the Khalifate, and the influence which these relations had upon the development of the one and the other.   It will be agreeable to the natural arrangement to take the former question first.

With a view to the better understanding of the position of Christianity and Mohammedanism at the very beginning of our inquiry, we have thought it advisable to point out in a preliminary sketch the development of Christianity in Spain previous to the period when the Moslems, fresh from their native deserts of Arabia and Africa, bearing the sword in one hand and the Koran in the other, possessed themselves of one of the fairest provinces of Christendom.   This having been already done, we can at once proceed to investigate the mutual relations of Christianity and Mohammedanism in Spain during the 300 years of the Khalifate of Cordova.

It was in fulfilment of a supposed prophecy of Mohammed's, and in obedience to the precepts of the Koran itself,

[1] Dozy, ii. 42.   [2] Cardonne, i. 106.

that the Arabs, having overrun Syria, Egypt, and Africa, passed over into Spain, and the war from the very first took the character of a jehad, or religious war—a character which it retained with the ever-increasing fanaticism of the combatants until every Mohammedan had been forced to abjure his creed, or been driven out of Spain. But, as we have seen, the conquest itself was singularly free from any outbursts of religious frenzy ; though of course there must have been many Christians, who laid down their lives in defence of all that was near and dear to them, in defence of their wives and their children, their homes and their country, their religion and their honour. One such instance at least has been recorded by the Arab historians,[1] when the Governor, and 400 of the garrison, of Cordova, after three months' siege in the church of St George, chose rather to be burnt in their hold than surrender upon condition either of embracing Islam, or paying tribute.

Omitting the story of the fabulous martyr Nicolaus, as being a tissue of errors and absurdities,[2] the first martyr properly so called was a certain bishop, named Anambad, who was put to death by Othman ibn abi Nesah (727-728) —a governor guilty of shedding much Christian blood, if Isidore is to be believed.[3]

Fifteen years later a Christian named Peter, pursuing very much the same tactics as the pseudo-martyrs in the next

[1] Al Makkari, i. 279, says : " This was the cause of the spot being called ever since the Kenisatu-l-haraki (the church of the burnt), as likewise of the great veneration in which it has always been held by the Christians, on account of the courage and endurance displayed in the cause of their religion by those who died in it."

[2] Florez, " España Sagr," xiv. 392.

[3] Isidore, sec. 58, "Munuza quia a sanguine Christianorum, quem ibidem innocentem fuderat, nimium erat crapulatus, et Anabadi, illustris episcopi, ... quem ipse cremaverat, valde exhaustus," etc. It is doubtful who this Munuza was, but probably Othman ibn abi Nesah, Governor of Spain.

century, brought about his own condemnation and death. He held a responsible post under Government, that of receiver of public imposts, and seems to have stood on terms of friendship with many of the Arab nobles. Perhaps he had been rather lax in his religious observances, or even disguised his Christianity from motives of interest. However, he fell sick, and thinking that his life was near its end, he called together his Moslem friends, and thanking them for showing their concern for him by coming, he proceeded, "But I desire you to be witnesses of this my last will. Whosoever believeth not on the Father, the Son, and the Holy Ghost, the Consubstantial Trinity, is blind in heart, and deserveth eternal punishment, as also doth Mohammed, your false prophet, the forerunner of Antichrist. Renounce, therefore, these fables, I conjure you this day, and let heaven and earth witness between us." Though greatly incensed, as was natural, the hearers resolved to take no notice of these and other like words, charitably supposing the sick man to be light-headed; but Peter, having unexpectedly recovered, repeated his former condemnation of Mohammed, cursing him, his book, and his followers. Thereupon he was executed, and we cannot be altogether surprised at it.[1]

Besides these two isolated cases of martyrdom, we do not find any more recorded until the reign of Abdurrahman II. (May 822-Aug. 852). In the second year of this king's reign, two Christians, John and Adulphus, making public profession of their faith, and denouncing Mohammed, were put to death on Sept. 17, 824.[2]

This is the first definite indication we have that the

[1] We give the account as Fleury, v. 88 (Bk. 42), gives it, but with great doubts as to its genuineness, no other writer that we have seen mentioning it.

[2] Florez, x. 358: Fleury, v. 487. They were buried in St Cyprian's Church, Cordova. See "De translatione martyrum Georgii, etc.," sec. 7.

toleration shown by the Moslems was beginning to be abused by their Christian subjects; and there can be no reasonable doubt that this ill-advised conduct on the part of the latter was the main cause of the so-called persecution which followed. But besides this fanaticism on the part of a small section of the subject Christians, there were other causes at work calculated to produce friction between the two peoples. During the century which had elapsed since the conquest, the Christians and Mohammedans, living side by side under the same government, and one which, considering the times in which it arose, was remarkable no less for its equity and moderation than for its external splendour and magnificence, had gradually been drawn closer together. Intermarriages had become frequent among them;[1] and these proved the fruitful cause of religious dissensions. Accordingly we find that the religious troubles in the reigns of Abdurrahman II. (822-852) and Mohammed I. (852-886) began with the execution of two children of mixed parents. Nunilo and Alodia were the children of a Moslem father and a Christian mother. Their father was a tolerant man, and, apparently, while he lived, permitted his children to profess the faith of their mother. On his death, the mother married again, and the new husband, being a bigoted Mohammedan, and actuated, as we may suppose, by the *odio vitrici*, immediately set about reclaiming his step-children to the true faith of Islam, his efforts in this direction leading him to ill-treat, even to torture,[2] the young confessors. His utmost endeavour to effect their conversion failing, he delivered them over to the judge on the charge of apostasy, and the judge to the executioner, by whom they were beheaded on Oct. 21, 840.[3]

[1] Due in part no doubt to the marriage of captives. See also below for "the maiden tribute," pp. 96, 97.　　[2] So Miss Yonge.

[3] This date is given by Morales, apud Migne, vol. cxv. p. 886, and by Fleury, v. 487, who accuse Eulogius, "Mem. Sanct.," ii. c. 10, of

Though there were some cases of martyrdom of this character, where the sufferers truly earned their title of martyrs,—and we may believe that all such cases have not been recorded—yet the vast majority of those which followed in the years 851-860 were of a different type. They were due to an outbreak of fanatical zeal on the part of a certain section of the Christians such as to overpower the spirit of toleration, which the Moslem authorities had so far shown in dealing with their Christian subjects, and to raise a corresponding tide of bigotry in the less enlightened, and therefore more intolerant, masses of the Mohammedans. The sudden mania for martyrdom which manifested itself at this time is certainly the most remarkable phenomenon of the kind that has been recorded in the annals of the Christian Church. There had been occasional instances before of Christians voluntarily offering themselves to undergo the penalty of the laws for the crime of being Christians. One such instance in the case of a Phrygian, named Quintus, had caused grave scandal to the Church of Smyrna; for, having gone before the proconsul and professed himself ready to die for the faith, when the reality of the death, which he courted, had been brought home to him by the sight of the wild beasts ready to rend him, the courage of the Phrygian had failed, and he had offered incense to the gods. Africa also had had her self-accused martyrs.

But the Spanish confessors have an interest over and above these, both by reason of their number and the constancy which they displayed in their self-imposed task. Not a single instance is recorded, though there may have been some such, where the would-be martyr from fear or any other cause forwent his crown. Moreover these martyrdoms, by dividing the Church on the question

being in error when he assigns the date 851. The Pseudo-Luitprand gives 951, vouching for this date as an eye-witness: "Me vivente, in castro Wergeti, id est Castellon, etc."

of their merit, whether, that is, the victims were to be ranked as true martyrs or not, and, giving rise to a written controversy on the subject, has supplied us with ample, if rather one-sided, materials for estimating the provocation given, and received, on either side.

As time went on, and the Christians and Moslems mingled more closely together in political and social life, the Church no doubt suffered some deterioration. Every interested motive was enlisted in favour of dropping as far as possible out of sight[1] those distinctive features of Christianity which might be calculated to give offence to the Moslems ; of conforming to all those Mohammedan customs, which are not in the Bible expressly forbidden to a Christian ;[2] and, generally, of emphasizing the points on which Christianity agrees with Mohammedanism, and ignoring those (far more important ones) in which they differ. The Moslems had no such reason for dissembling their convictions, or modifying their tenets. Consequently a spiritual paralysis was creeping upon the Church, which threatened in the course of time, if not checked, to destroy the very life of Christianity throughout the peninsula. The case of Africa, from which Islam had extirpated Christianity, showed that this was no imaginary danger. But Spain had this advantage over Africa : it contained a free Christian community which had never passed under the Moslem yoke, where the fire of Christianity, in danger of being swept away by the devouring flames of Mohammedanism, might be nursed and cherished, till it could again blaze forth with its former brilliancy.

Yet in Mohammedan Spain religious fervour was not wholly vanished : it was still to be found among the clergy, and specially among the dwellers in convents. Monks and nuns, severed from all worldly influences, in the silence of

---

[1] See below, p. 72, note 5.   [2] *E.g.*, circumcision.

their cloisters, would read the lives of the Saints[1] of old, and meditate upon their glorious deeds, and the miracles which their faith had wrought. They would brood over such texts as, " Ye shall be brought before rulers and kings for My sake ; "[2] and, "Every one who shall confess Me before men, him will I also confess before My Father, which is in Heaven ; "[3] till they brought themselves to believe that it was their imperative duty to bring themselves before rulers and kings, and not only to confess Christ, but to revile Mohammed.

However, the reproach of fanatical self-destruction will not apply, as the apologists of their doings have not failed to point out, to the first two victims that suffered in this persecution.

Perfectus,[4] a priest of Cordova, who had been brought up in the school attached to the church of St Acislus, on going out one day to purchase some necessaries for domestic use, was stopped by some of the Moslems in the street, and asked to give his opinion of their Prophet. What led them to make this strange request, we are not told,[5] but stated thus barely it certainly gives us the impression that it was intended to bring the priest into trouble. For it was a well-known law in Moslem countries that if any one cursed a Mohammedan, he was to be scourged,[6] if he struck him, killed : the latter penalty also awaiting any one who spoke evil of Mohammed, and extending even to a Mussulman

---

[1] See Dozy, ii. 112.   [2] St Mark xiii. 9.   [3] St Matt. x. 32.

[4] Eulogius, "Mem. Sanct.," ii., ch. i. secs. 1-4 : Alvar, "Indic. Lum.," sec. 3.   [5] See, however, Appendix A, p. 158.

[6] Alvar, " Ind. Lum.," sec. 6.   " Ecce enim lex publica pendet, et legalis iussa per omnem regnum eorum discurrit, ut, qui blasphematur, flagellatur, et qui percusserit occidatur." Neander V., p. 464, note, points out that " blasphemaverit " refers to cursing Moslems, not Mohammed. Eul., "Mem. Sanct.," Pref., sec. 5, "Irrefragibilis manet sententia, animadverti debere in eos qui talia de ipso non verentur profiteri." On hearing of Isaac's death the king published a reminder on this law.

ruler, if he heard the blasphemy without taking notice of it.[1]
Perfectus, therefore, being aware of this law, gave a cautious[2]
answer, declining to comply with their request until they
swore that he should receive no hurt in consequence of what
he might say. On their giving the required stipulation, he
quoted the words, "For there shall arise false Christs and
false prophets, and shall show great signs and wonders;
insomuch that if it were possible they shall deceive the very
elect,"[3] and proceeded to speak of Mohammed in the usual
fashion, as a lying impostor and a dissolute adulterer, concluding with the words, "Thus hath he, the encourager of all
lewdness, and the wallower in his own filthy lusts, delivered
you all over to the indulgence of an everlasting sensuality."
This ill-advised abuse of one, whom the Moslems revere
as we revere Christ, and the ungenerous advantage taken
of the oath, which they had made, naturally incensed his
hearers to an almost uncontrollable degree. They respected
their promise, however, and refrained from laying hands
on him at that time, with the intention, says Eulogius, of
revenging themselves on a future occasion.[4]

If this was so, the opportunity soon presented itself, and
Perfectus, being abroad on an errand similar to the previous
one, was met[5] by his former interrogators, who, on the
charge of reviling Mohammed, and doing despite to their
religion, dragged him before the Kadi. Being questioned,
his courage at first failed him, and he withdrew his words.
He was then imprisoned to await further examination at the
end of the month, which happened to be the Ramadhan or
fast month. In prison the priest repented his weakness,
and when brought again before the judge on the Mohammedan Easter, he recanted his recantation, adding, "I have

---

[1] See p. 91.   [2] Alvar, "Ind. Lum.," sec. 3, calls it a timid answer.
[3] Matt. xxiv. 24.
[4] "Accensum ultionis furorem in corde ad perniciem eius reponunt."
Eulogius, l.l.
[5] "Dolo circumventum," says Alvar, "Ind. Lum.," sec. 4.

cursed and do curse your prophet, a messenger not of God, but of Satan, a dealer in witchcraft, an adulterer, and a liar." He was immediately led off for execution, but before his death prophesied that of the King's minister, Nazar, within a year of his own. He was beheaded on April 18, 850.[1] The apologists, on insufficient evidence, describe the death of two Moslems, who were drowned the same day in the river, as a manifest judgement of Heaven for the murder of Perfectus.[2]

The example set by Perfectus did not bear fruit at once, but no doubt the evidence which it gave of the ease and comparative painlessness, with which a martyr's crown could be obtained, was not lost upon the brooding and zealous spirits living in solitary retreats and trying by a life of religious devotion to cut themselves off from the seductive pleasures of an active life.

The next victim, a little more than a year later, was a petty tradesman, named John,[3] who does not seem to have courted his own fate. He had aroused the animosity of his Moslem rivals by a habit which he had contracted of pronouncing the name of the Prophet in his market trans-actions, taking his name, as they thought, in vain, and with a view to attracting buyers.[4] John, being taxed with this, with ill-timed pleasantry retorted, "Cursed be he who wishes to name your Prophet." He was haled before the

---

[1] Johannes Vasaeus places this persecution (by a manifest error) in 950, under Abdurrahman III., stating at the same time that some writers placed it in 850, but, as it appeared to him, wrongly: "Abdurrahman Halihatan rex Cordobae movit duodecimam persecu-tionem in Christianos." [2] Eulog., "Mem. Sanct." ii., ch. i. sec. 5.

[3] Eugolius, "Mem. Sanct." i. sec. 9; and Alvar, Ind. Lum. sec. 5.

[4] So Eulogius, l.l., and Dozy, ii., 129. Alvar's account (l.l.) is not very intelligible: "Parvipendens nostrum prophetam, semper eius nomen in derisione frequentas, et mendacium tuum per iuramenta nostrae religionis, ut tibi videtur, falsa auribus te ignorantium Christianum esse semper confirmas."

Kadi, and, after receiving 400 stripes,[1] was thrown into prison. Subsequently he was taken thence and driven through the city riding backwards on an ass, while a crier was sent before him through the Christian quarters, proclaiming: "Such shall be the punishment of those, that speak evil of the Prophet of God."

So far we have had cases, where the charge of persecution, brought by the apologists of the martyrs against the Moslems, can be more or less sustained, but the next instance is of a different character. Isaac,[2] a monk of Tabanos, and descended from noble and wealthy ancestors, was born in 824, and by his knowledge of Arabic, attained in early life to the position of an exceptor, or scribe,[3] but gave up his appointment at the age of twenty, in order to enter the monastery of Tabanos, which his uncle and aunt, Jeremiah and Elizabeth, had founded near Cordova.

Roused by the tale of Perfectus' death and John's sufferings, he voluntarily went before the Kadi, and, pretending to be an "enquirer," begged him to expound to him the doctrines of Islam. The Kadi, congratulating himself on the prospect of such a promising convert, gravely complied; when Isaac, answering him in fluent Arabic, said: "He has lied unto you—may the curse of Heaven consume him!—who full of all wickedness has led astray so many men, and doomed them with himself to the lowest deep of hell. Filled with Satan, and practising Satanic arts, he hath given his followers a drink of deadly wine, and will without doubt expiate his guilt with everlasting damnation." Hearing these,

---

[1] Or, according to Eulogius, 500.

[2] Eulog., "Mem. Sanct.," ii. ch. ii. sec. 1, also Pref., secs. 2 ff. After his death Isaac was credited with having performed miracles from his earliest years. He was said to have spoken three times in his mother's womb (cp. a similar fable about Jesus in the Koran, c. iii. verse 40), and when a child, to have embraced, unhurt, a globe of fire from Heaven.

[3] Not, as Florez, a tax-gatherer.

and other like *chaste*[1] utterances, the judge listened in a sort of stupor of rage and astonishment, feelings which even found vent in tears ; till, his indignation passing all control, he struck the monk in the face, who then said, "Dost thou strike that which is made in the image of God?"[2]   The assessors of the Kadi also reproached him for striking a prisoner, their law being that one who is worthy of death should not suffer other indignities.   The Kadi, having now recovered his self-command, gave his decision, that Isaac, whether drunk or mad, had committed a crime which, by an express law of Mohammed's, merited condign punishment. He was accordingly beheaded, and, his body being burnt, his ashes were cast into the river (June 3, 851).   This was done to prevent the Christians from carrying off his body, and preserving it for the purpose of working miracles.[3]

Isaac's conduct and fate, Eulogius tells us, electrified the people, who were amazed at the *newness* of the thing.[4]   It was at this point that Eulogius himself began to shew his sympathy with these fanatical doings by encouraging and helping others to follow Isaac's example.

The number of misguided men and women that now came forward and threw their lives away is certainly remarkable, and seems to have struck the Moslems as perfectly unaccountable.   The Arabs themselves were as brave men as the world has ever seen, and, by the very ordinances of their faith, were bound to adventure their lives for their religion in actual human conflict with infidel foes, yet they were unable to conceive how any man in his senses could willingly deprive himself of life in such a way as could do no service to the cause, religious or other, which he had at

---

[1] Eulogius, "Mem. Sanct.," Pref., sec. 5, "*Ore pudico* summisque reverentiae ausibus viribusque."   [2] Cp. Acts xxiii. 3.

[3] Eulog., "Lib. Apolog.," sec. 35, mentions a proposed edict of the authorities, visiting the seeker of relics with severer penalties.

[4] See Eulog., Letter to Alvar, apud Florez., xi. 290.

heart. They were quite unable to appreciate that intense antagonism towards the world and its perilous environment, which Christianity teaches; that spirit of renouncement of the vanities, nay, even of the duties of life, which prompted men and women to immure themselves in cloisters and retreats, far from all spheres of human usefulness. Life under these circumstances had naturally little to make it worth the living, and became all the more easy to relinquish, when death, in itself a thing to be desired, was further invested with the glories of martyrdom.

The example of Isaac was therefore followed within two days by a monk named Sanctius[1] or Sancho, who was executed on June 5th. Three days later were beheaded Peter, a priest of Ecija; Walabonsus, a deacon of Ilipa; Sabinianus and Wistremundus, monks of St Zoilus; Habentius, a monk of St Christopher's Church at Cordova; while Jeremiah,[2] uncle of Isaac, was scourged to death. Their bodies were burned, and the ashes cast into the river.

Sisenandus of Badajos[3] found a similar fate on July 16th: four days subsequently Paul, a deacon of St Zoilus, gave himself up; and the same number of days later, Theodomir, a monk of Carmona: all of whom were beheaded.

[1] Eulog., "Mem. Sanct.," ii. c. 3. [2] *Ibid.*, c. iv.
[3] After his martyrdom he procured the release from prison of Tiberias, priest of Beja! Eulog., "Mem. Sanct.," ii. c. vi.

———o———

CHAPTER IV.

FANATICISM OF THE MARTYRS.

THE next candidates for martyrdom were two young and beautiful girls, whose history we learn from their patron, Eulogius, who seems to have regarded one of these maidens, Flora, with a Platonic love mingled with a sort of religious devotion.

Flora,[1] the daughter of a Moslem father and a Christian mother, was born at Cordova. She is said to have practised abstinence even in her cradle. At first she was brought up as a Moslem, and lived in conformity with that faith, until, being converted to Christianity about eight years before this time, and finding the intolerance of her father and her brother unbearable, she deserted her home. But when her brother, in his efforts to discover and reclaim her, persecuted many Christian families, whom he suspected of conniving at her escape, she voluntarily surrendered herself to him, saying, " Here am I whom you seek, and for whose sake you persecute the people of God. I am a Christian. Do your best to annul that confession : none of your torments will be able to overcome my faith." Her brother, after trying in vain, by alternate threats and blandishments, to bring her back from her error, finally dragged her before the Kadi ; and he, hearing her brother's accusation, and her own confession, ordered her to be barbarously beaten, and then given up nearly dead to her brother. She managed, however, to recover, and escaped under angelic guidance.[2] Shortly afterwards, while praying in a church, she was found by Maria, sister of Walabonsus

---

[1] " Life of Flora and Maria," by Eulogius, secs. 3 ff.
[2] *Ibid.*, sec. 8.   " Agelico comitante meatu."

above-mentioned,[1] who had been martyred a few months previously. Their father, being a Christian, converted his unbelieving wife. They came to live at Froniano, near Cordova, and their daughter was educated at the nunnery of Cuteclara, near the city, under the care of the abbess, Artemia. Brooding over her brother's martyrdom, and perhaps, as was so often the case, seeing his glorified spirit in a vision, she left the cloister, determining to follow in his saintly footsteps. While on her way to give herself up, she turned aside into a church to pray, and found Flora there.

. Together, then, did these devoted girls go forth[2] to curse Mohammed, of whom they probably knew next to nothing, and lose their own lives. The judge, however, pitying their youth and beauty, merely imprisoned them. News of his sister's imprisonment being brought to Flora's brother, he induced the judge to make a further examination of her, and she was brought out of prison before the Kadi, who, pointing to her brother, asked her if she knew him. Flora answered that she did—as her brother according to the flesh. "How is it, then," asked the judge, "that he remains a good Moslem, while you have apostatized?" She answered that God had enlightened her; and, on professing herself ready to repeat her former denunciations of the Prophet, she was again remanded to prison. Here she and Maria are threatened with being thrown upon the streets as prostitutes[3]—a punishment far worse than the

[1] "Life of Flora and Maria," sec. 11. Lane Poole, "Moors in Spain," says, "Sister of Isaac."

[2] Eulog. to Alvar, i. sec. 2 ; "Life of Flora and Maria," by Eulog., sec. 12.

[3] *Ibid.*, sec. 13, and Eulog., "Doc. Mart.," sec. 4. Eulogius tried to lessen the terror of this threat by pointing out that "non polluit mentem aliena corruptio, quam non foedat propria delectatis,"—a poor consolation, but the only one ! He does not seem to have known—or surely he would have quoted it—the express injunction of the Koran (xxiv. verse 35):—"Compel not your maidservants to prostitute

easy death they had desired.   This shakes their constancy ;
when they find an unexpected comforter in Eulogius himself, who is now imprisoned for being an encourager and
inciter of defiance to the laws.   It is strange that he should
have been allowed to carry on in the prison itself the very
work for which he had been imprisoned.   The support
of Eulogius enabled these tender maidens to stand firm
through another examination, and the judge, proving too
merciful, or too good a Moslem, to carry out the above-
mentioned threat, they were led forth to die (November 24,
851).   Before their death they had promised Eulogius to
intercede before the throne of God for his release, which
accordingly is brought to pass six days after their own
execution.[1]

An interval of only a little more than a month elapsed
before Gumesindus, a priest of the district called Campania,
near Cordova, and Servus Dei, a monk, suffered death in
the same way (January 13, 852).[2]

There was now a pause for six months in the race for
martyrdom, and it seemed as if the Church had come to
its right mind upon this subject.   This, however, was far
from being the case.   Hitherto the victims had been
almost without exception priests, monks, and nuns ; but
the next martyrs afford us instances of married couples
claiming a share in this doubtful honour.   These were
Aurelius, son of a Moslem father and a Christian mother,
and his wife Sabigotha (or Nathalia), the daughter of
Moslem parents, whose father dying, her mother married
a Christian and was converted ; and Felix and his wife
Liliosa.[3]   It would seem that with all the harm that was
themselves, if they be willing to live chastely . . . but, if any shall
compel them thereto, verily God will be gracious and merciful unto such
women after their compulsion."

[1] Eulog., letter to Alvar, Florez, xi. 295.   Fleury, v. 100.
[2] Eulogius, " Mem. Sanct.," ii. c. ix.
[3] *Ibid.*, ii. ch. x., secs. 1, 2.

done by this outbreak of fanaticism, some good was also effected in awaking the worldly-minded adherents of Christianity from the spiritual torpor into which they were sinking; for these new martyrs were of the class of hidden [1] Christians, who were now shamed into avowing their real creed.[2] Yet surely it had been far better if they had been content to live like Christians instead of dying like suicides. In their case, indeed, we find no sudden irresistible impulse driving them to defy the laws, but a slowly-matured conviction that it was their duty, disregarding all human ties, to give themselves up to death. In this resolution they were fortified by the advice and encouragement of Eulogius and Alvar,[3] the latter of whom prudently warns Aurelius to make sure that his courage is sufficient to stand the trial.[4] Sabigotha is persuaded to accompany her husband in his self-destruction, her natural reluctance to leave her children being overcome by Eulogius,[5] who recommends that they should be given over to the care of a monastery. A seasonable vision, in which Flora and Maria appear to her, clenches her purpose.

Meanwhile a foreign monk from Bethlehem, who, being sent on business connected with his monastery to Africa, had crossed over in Spain, impelled by the wild enthusiasm there prevailing, determined to offer himself as a candidate for martyrdom with the four persons above mentioned.

They then take counsel together how they may best effect their purpose, there being evidently enough difficulty in

[1] See below, p. 72.

[2] Aurelius was roused from his religious dissimulation by seeing the sufferings of John. See Eulog., "Mem. Sanct.," ii. c. x. sec. 5.

[3] *Ibid.*, sec. 18.

[4] This would lead us to suppose that the courage of some *had* failed.

[5] Eulogius comments :—" O admirabilis ardor divinus, quo filiorum affectus respuitur !" The parents not only desert their children, but give away most of their goods to the poor, thereby making their own children of the number.

procuring martyrdom for themselves to shew the statements of the apologists, that there was a fierce persecution raging, to be at least much exaggerated, if not entirely without foundation. The plan decided upon, which the devisers audaciously attributed to the suggestion of God,[1] was that the women should go forth unveiled and with hurried steps to the church, in the hope that such an unwonted sight would direct attention to them, and occasion the arrest of the whole number. It fell out as desired, and they were all brought before the judge, and interrogated with the usual result, except that the judge on this occasion dismissed them with scornful anger.[2] But George, disappointed at his untoward clemency, as they were being led away broke out with,[3] "Can you not go down to hell without seeking to drag us also thither as your companions?"

This incoherent abuse naturally incensed the soldiers, as it was no doubt intended that it should. Accordingly the prisoners were dragged again before the Kadi, who asked them in a mild tone of remonstrance, why they had abandoned the faith of Islam,[4] and refused to live, promising them at the same time great rewards, if they would become Moslems again. On their refusal they were remanded for two days, which seemed a very long time, so eager were they to die. They pass the time with singing hymns, and are blessed with visits of angels and miraculous signs. Their chains drop off, and the gaolers dare not again bind

---

[1] Eulog., "Mem. Sanct.," ii. sec. 27. "Omnes in communi coepimus *cogitare quomodo ad desideratam perveniremus coronam:* et ita *Domino dispensante* visum est nobis ut fugerent sorores nostrae revelatis vultibus ad ecclesiam si forte nos alligandi daretur occasio, et ita factum est."

[2] *Ibid.*, sec. 29. "Exite quibus vita praesens taedium est, et mors pro gloria computatur."

[3] *Ibid.*, sec. 30. "An non poteritis vos infernalia claustra adire, nisi nos comites habeatis? Numquid sine nobis aeterna vos cruciamina non adurent?"   [4] *Ibid.*, sec. 31.

those whom Christ Himself had loosed.[1] The authorities, now as ever, anxious if possible to avoid extreme penalties, determine to release George, because they had not themselves[2] heard his blasphemy. He baulks their merciful intention by repeating his words on the spot, and he is accordingly led forth and beheaded with the others (July 27, 852).

Within a month Christopher,[3] a monk of Rojana, and of Arab lineage, and Leovigild, a monk of Fraga, both being places near Cordova, are executed for the same offence and in the same manner, their dead bodies being nailed to stakes. While taking the air in his palace,[4] the king saw these bodies, and ordered them to be burnt, and the ashes scattered in the river. The same night Abdurrahman II. was struck down with apoplexy, and the martyrs' friends hailed it as a manifest judgment from Heaven.

He was succeeded by Mohammed I. (852-886), a less capable and more bigoted ruler than his father. No sooner was he on the throne than Emila, a deacon, and Jeremiah a priest of St Cyprian's church, near Cordova, following in

---

[1] Eulog., "Mem. Sanct.," sec. 32.

[2] *Ibid.*, sec. 33. "Ipsi optimates et priores palatii." George, being a foreigner, could not be charged with apostasy like the others.

[3] *Ibid.*, ii. c. xi. Alvar's Life of Eul., iv. 12.

[4] On a "sublime solarium," Eul., "Mem. Sanct.," c. ii. sec. 2. See Ortiz, "Compendio," iii. 52 (apud Buckle, ii. 442, note.) "En lo mas cruel de los tormentos subió Abderramen un dia á las azutens ó galerias de su Palacio. Descubrió desde alli los cuerpos de los Santos marterizados en los patibulos y atravesados con los palos, mandó los quemasen todos paraque no quedase reliquia cumplióse luego la órdsa ; pero aquel impio probó bien presto los rigores de la venganza divina que volviá por la sangre derramada de sus Santos. Improvisamente se le pegó la lengua al paladar y fauces : cerróssle la boca, y no pudo pronunciar una palabra, ni dar un gemido. Conduxeronle, sus criados à la cama, murio aguella misma noche, y antes de apagarse las hoqueras en que ardian los santos cuerpos, entró la infeliz alma de Abderramen en los etemos fuegos del infierno."

the footsteps of so many predecessors, came before the Kadi, and reviled Mohammed,—the former being enabled to do this with the more point and effect, as he was to a remarkable degree master of the Arabic language.[1] Emila and Jeremiah won the prize they coveted, and were put to death (September 15, 852). The customary prodigy occurred after the execution, in describing which the pious Eulogius breaks into metre, saying, "Athletas cecidisse pios elementa fatentur."

On the following day occurred an outrage which the most bigoted partizans of the martyrs must have blushed to record. Two eunuchs, Rogel, a monk of Parapanda, near Elvira, and Servio Deo, a eunuch of foreign extraction, forced their way into a mosque, and by way of preaching—as they said—to the assembled worshippers, they reviled their Prophet and their religion.[2] Being set upon and nearly torn in pieces by the infuriated congregation, they were rescued by the Kadi, who imprisoned them till such time as their sentence should be declared. They were condemned to have their hands and feet cut off, and be beheaded; which sentence was carried into effect.[3]

Upon this fresh provocation the fury and apprehension of the king knew no bounds. He might well be pardoned for thinking that this defiance of the laws, and religious fanaticism, could only mean a widespread disaffection and conspiracy against the Moslem rule. In fact, as we shall see, the Christians of Toledo raised the banner of revolt in favour of their Cordovan brethren at this very time. Mohammed therefore seems to have meditated a real persecution, such as should extirpate Christianity in his

---

[1] Eulog., "Mem. Sanct.," ii. c. xii. Arabic boasts a larger vocabulary of abuse than most languages: see the account of Prof. Palmer's death in his Life by Besant.　　[2] *Ibid.*, c. xiii. secs. 1, 2.

[3] Eul. (l.l), adds: "Et ipsa gentilitas tali spectaculo stupefacta nescio quid de Christianismo indulgentius sentiebat."

dominions.[1]   He is said even to have given orders for a
general massacre of the males among the Christians, and
for the slavery, or worse, of the women, if they did not
apostatize.[2]   But the dispassionate advice of his councillors
saved the king from this crime.   They pointed out that no
men of any intelligence, education, or rank among the
Christians had taken part in the doings of the zealots,
and that the whole body of Christians ought not to be cut
off, since their actions were not directed by any individual
leader.   Other advisers seem to have diverted the king from
his project of a wholesale massacre by encouraging him
to proceed legally against the Christians with the utmost
rigour, and by this means to cow them into submission.[3]

These strong measures apparently produced some effect,
for no other executions are recorded for a period of nine
months ; when Fandila, a priest of Tabanos,[4] and chosen by
the monks of St Salvator's monastery to be one of their
spiritual overseers, came forward and reviled the Prophet :
whereupon he was imprisoned and subsequently beheaded
(June 13, 853).   His fate awakened the dormant fanaticism
of Anastasius,[5] a priest of St Acislus' church ; of Felix, a

---

[1] Eulog., "Mem. Sanct.," ii. c. xii.   "Non iam solummodo de
mortibus resistentium sibi excogitare coeperunt, verum etiam totam
extirpare ecclesiam ruminarunt.   Quoniam nimio terrore tot hominum
recurrentium ad martyrium concussa gentilitas regni sui arbitrabatur
imminere excidium, cum tali etiam praecinctos virtute parvulos
videret."   A similar project is attributed (mistakenly, without doubt)
to Abdurrahman.

[2] *Ibid.*, iii. c. vii. sec. 4.   "Iusserat enim omnes Christianos
generali sententia perdere, feminasque publico distractu disperdere."
Cp. also Alvar, Life of Eul., iv. 12.   "Rex Mahomad incredibili rabie
et effrenata sententia Christicolum genus delere funditus cogitabat."

[3] *Ibid.*, "Multi insaniam modificare nitentes per trucem voluntatis
iniquae officium diversis et exquisitis occasionibus gregem Christi
impetere tentaverunt."

[4] *Ibid.*, iii. c. vii. secs. 1, 2.   Fleury, v. 520, says he was a monk
of Guadix.   [5] *Ibid.*, ch. viii. secs. 1, 2.

Gaetulian monk of Alcala de Henares; and of Digna, a virgin of St Elizabeth's nunnery at Tabanos (the latter being strengthened in her resolve by a celestial vision), who, pursuing the usual plan, are beheaded the following day; their example being followed by Benildis, a matron (June 15).[1]

The cloisters of Tabanos had furnished so many fanatics that the Government now suppressed the place, removing the nuns and shutting them up to prevent others giving themselves up.[2] One of these however, Columba,[3] sister of Elizabeth and of the abbot Martin, contrived to escape. This Columba had persisted in remaining a virgin, in spite of her mother's efforts to make her marry, which only ceased when the mother died. She now gave herself up and was beheaded (September 17).

Just one month later Pomposa,[4] from the monastery of St Salvator, Pegnamellar, suffered the same fate. Then there was a pause in these executions, which was not broken till July 11th of the following year, when Abundius, a priest, was martyred. He seems to have really deserved the name of martyr, for he was given up to the authorities by the treachery of others,[5] and did not seek martyrdom.

Another similar period elapsed before Amator, a priest of Tucci (Tejada); Peter, a monk of Cordova; and Ludovic, a brother of Paul, the deacon, beheaded four years before, shared the same fate (April 30, 855).[6]

After nearly a year Witesindus, a repentant renegade; Elias, an old priest of Lusitania; and Paul and Isidore, young monks, gave themselves up to execution[7] (April 17, 856.) In June of that year a more venerable victim was,

---

[1] Eulog., " Mem. Sanct.," iii. ch. ix.   [2] So Miss Yonge.

[3] Eulog., " Mem. Sanct.," iii. c. x. secs. 1, 2.   [4] *Ibid.*, c. xi.

[5] *Ibid.*, ch. xii. " Quorundam commento vel fraude gentilium ad martyrium furore pertractum."

[6] *Ibid.*, ch. xiii.   [7] *Ibid.*, cc. xiv. xv.

like Abundius, betrayed to his destruction. This was Argimirus, an old monk, once Censor of Cordova (June 28).[1] Exactly one month later Aurea, a virgin and sister of the brothers John and Adulphus, whose martyrdom has been already mentioned, was brought before the magistrate. Descended from one of the noblest Arab families,[2] she had long been left unmolested, though her apostasy to Christianity was well known. She was now frightened into temporary submission; but soon repenting of her compliance, and avowing herself truly a Christian, she gained a martyr's crown (July 29).

The next example affords a similar instance of real persecution. Ruderic,[3] a priest, whose brother was a Moslem, unadvisedly intervened as a peacemaker, in a quarrel, in which his brother was engaged. With the usual fate of peacemakers, he was set upon by both parties, and nearly killed. In fact his brother supposed him to be quite dead, and had the body carried through the town, proclaiming that his brother had become a Mussulman before his death.[4] However, Ruderic recovered, and made his escape, but being obliged to return to Cordova, met his brother, who immediately brought him before the Kadi on a charge of apostasy. His life and liberty were promised to him if he would only acknowledge that Christ was merely man, and that Mohammed was the messenger of God. On refusing, he is imprisoned, and finds in prison a certain Salomon, also charged with apostasy from Islam. The two fellow-prisoners contract a great friendship and are consequently separated. After a third exhortation, they are condemned to death, but not before the judge had done

---

[1] Eulog., " Mem. Sanct.," iii. c. xv., " Quorundam ethnicorum dolo vel odio circumventus."

[2] *Ibid.*, xvii. sec. 1, " Grandi fastu Arabicae traducis exornabatur."

[3] Eulog., " Lib. Apol.," sec. 21 ff.

[4] So the Inquisitors in Spain used to pretend that their victims had abjured their errors before being burnt.

his best to bribe them to forego their purpose by offers of honour and rewards.[1] They were executed March 13, 857, and their bodies thrown into the river—even the stones sprinkled with their blood being taken up and cast into the water, lest the Christians should preserve them as relics. Ruderic's body was washed on shore, fresh as when killed; while Salomon, not being equally fortunate, informed a devout Christian in a vision, where his body lay in a tamarisk thicket near the town of Nymphianum.

Hitherto the aider and abettor of these martyrdoms had himself contrived to escape the penalty, which he had urged others to brave. Whether this was due to any unworthy fear of death on his part is not clear, but it may have been owing to the respect in which he was held by the Moslem authorities. To these he was well known as a man of irreproachable character and unaffected piety, and several Arabs of high rank, who were his personal friends, shewed themselves anxious to screen him from the effects of his folly. Eulogius[2] was descended from a Senatorial family of Cordova, and was educated at the Church of St Zoilus, where he devoted himself to ecclesiastical studies, and soon surpassed his contemporaries in learning. With his friend Alvar he sat at the feet of Speraindeo, an eminent abbot in the province of Baetica. Besides a sister Anulo, Eulogius had two brothers engaged in trade, and another brother, Joseph, who seems to have been in government employ.[3]

Eulogius became early noted for his practice of asceticism, and his desire for the life of a monk,[4] and for the glory of

---

[1] Eul., "Lib. Apol.," sec. 27.

[2] Life by Alvar, c. i. sec. 2.

[3] Eul. ad Wiliesindum, sec. 8, "Joseph, quem saeva tyranni indignatio eo tempore a principatu dejecerat:" unless this is a metaphorical allusion to Joseph in Egypt.

[4] Life by Alvar, sec. 3, "Ne virtus animi curis Saecularibus enervaretur, quotidie ad caelestia cupiens volare corporea sarcina gravabatur."

martyrdom.　When strong measures were taken by the authorities, in concert witth Reccafredus, Bishop of Seville, to stamp out the mania for martyrdom by threats, stripes, and imprisonment, though many were frightened into submission, Eulogius, Alvar tells us,[1] remained firm, in spite of his being singled out as an "incentor martyrum" by a certain Gomez, who was a temporising Christian in the king's service.[2]

There is no doubt that Eulogius did all he could to interfere with and check that amalgamation of the Christians and Arabs which he saw going on round him.　Believing that such close relations between the peoples tended to the spiritual degradation of Christianity, he set himself deliberately to embitter those relations, and, as far as he could, to make a good understanding impossible.　To discourage the learning of Arabic by the Christians, he brought back with him from a journey to Pampluna the classical writings of Virgil, Horace (Satires), Juvenal, and Augustine's "De Civitate Dei."

At the time when these martyrdoms took place, Eulogius was a priest, but for some reason he tried to abstain from officiating at the mass on the ground that he was himself a great sinner.[3]　However, his ecclesiastical superior[4] (? Saul, Bishop of Cordova), soon made him take a different view of

---

[1] "Hic inadibilis (=firm) nunquam vacillare vel tenui est visus susurro."—Life by Alvar, sec. 5.

[2] This man, says Alvar, sec. 6, by a divine judgment, lost his hold on the Christian faith, which he thus scrupled not to attack.　See below, p. 72.

[3] He pleads his "delicti onera," ch. i. sec. 7.　Perhaps he was infected with one of the "Migetian errors" of the previous century, which was that "priests must be saints."　Saul, Bishop of Cordova (850-861), in a letter to another bishop (Florez, xi. 156-163), refers with disapproval to those (? Eulogius) who held that "sacramenta tunc esse solum modo sancta, cum sanctorum fuerint manibus praelibata;" and he quotes Augustine and Isidore against the error.

[4] Pontifex proprius.

the question by threatening him with anathema if he neglected his duty any longer.   Coming forward as a prominent champion of the extreme party in the Church, he was
imprisoned in 851, where he wrote treatises in favour of the
martyrs, and was released, as we have seen, by the interces-
sion of Flora and Maria on November 29th of that year.

In 858,[1] on the death of Wistremirus, he was chosen by
the votes of the people[2] to succeed him as Bishop of Toledo;
but from some cause, perhaps by the intervention of the
Moslems, he was prevented from occupying his see.   The
people then determined to have no bishop, if they might
not have him.[3]   Yet, adds the pious Alvar, he got his
bishopric after all, for "all holy men are bishops, though
not all bishops holy men."

In the following year he was again imprisoned as being
a disturber of the public peace, but as on a former occasion
he had been allowed to support and encourage Flora and
Maria, so now was he permitted to finish in prison a book in
defence of the martyrs,[4] which had the direct tendency of
inciting others to go and do likewise.   .The occasion of
Eulogius' second imprisonment was as follows :—Leocritia,
a maiden of Arab extraction and of noble birth,[5] had been
secretly baptised by Liliosa, the wife of Felix.   Her parents,
learning her apostasy, cruelly ill-treated, and even beat her,
in order to make her renounce Christ.   She naturally turned
to Eulogius and his sister Anulo for advice in her afflictions,
expressing a wish to escape to a part of Spain where the
Christian worship was free.   As a first step to this, she
leaves her parents under pretence of going to a wedding,
and takes refuge with Eulogius.   Her parents, furious at

---

[1] " Life of Eul.," Alvar, ii. sec. 10.   [2] " Communis electio."
[3] Fleury, v. 547, says another bishop was elected in Eulogius' life-
time ; but Alvar's words are "Alium sibi eo vivente interdixerunt
eligere."   [4] See Eulog., Letter to Alvar, Florez, xi. 295.
[5] Alvar, Life of Eulog., i. sec. 13.

her escape, get all sorts of people imprisoned on the charge
of aiding her; and she is at last betrayed and surprised at
the house of her protector.　They are both dragged before
the Kadi, who asks Eulogius angrily why he persists in defying the laws in this way.[1]　The bishop defends himself by
pleading that Christian clergy are bound to impart a knowledge of their religion, if asked, as he had been by Leocritia.[2]　The judge then threatens to have him scourged,
but Eulogius, preferring death to so painful and degrading
a punishment, repeats the lesson which he had taught to so
many others, and reviles Mohammed.　Even so the judge
shows a disposition to treat him with leniency, and he is
remanded to prison with Leocritia.

When brought up again before the royal Council,[3] an in-
fluential friend makes a last effort to save him, saying:
" Fools and idiots rush on their own destruction, but what
induces you, a man of approved wisdom and blameless
character, in defiance of all natural instincts, to throw away
your life in this manner? "　He urges Eulogius to say but
one word of concession in the hour of peril, promising that
he should afterwards be free to exercise his religion as he
pleased, without let or hindrance.　But the bishop could
hardly turn back now, and he rejected all such offers with
the ejaculation, " If they only knew the joy that awaits us
on high ! "

On his way to execution, when struck by one of the by-
standers on one cheek, he turned the other meekly to the
striker.　He was beheaded on March 11, 859, and Leocritia
four days later.　Miraculous appearances honoured the body
of the martyred bishop, which was buried in the Church of
St Genesius, whence it was translated in the next year to his

---

[1] Alvar, " Life of Eulog.," i. secs. 14, 15.
[2] This kind of proselytism was not held to be a capital crime by the
Moslems.　See Dozy, ii. 171.
[3] Alvar, " Life of Eul.," v. sec. 15.　Fleury v. 548.

own church of St Zoilus, and in 883 was given up, together with that of Leocritia, to Alphonso III. (866-910) by express stipulation.

————o————

CHAPTER V.

CONTROVERSY CONCERNING THE MARTYRS.

WITH the death of Eulogius the series of voluntary martyrdoms comes to an end, and it will be convenient at this point to consider the whole question of the relation of the Church to the civil power, and how far those "confessors," who were put to death under the circumstances already related, were entitled to the name of martyrs. Unfortunately the evidence we have on the subject is drawn almost entirely from the apologists of their doings, and therefore may fairly be suspected of some bias. Yet even from them can be shown conclusively enough that no real persecution was raging in Mohammedan Spain at this time, such as to justify the extreme measures adopted by the party of zealots.

If we except the cases of John and Adulphus, and of Nunilo and Alodia, the date of which is doubtful, there is not a single recorded instance of a Christian being put to death for his religion by the Arabs in Spain before the middle of the ninth century. The Muzarabes,[1] as the Christians living under the Arabs were called, enjoyed a remarkable degree of freedom in the exercise of their religion—the services and rites of the Church being conducted

[1] De Gayangos on Al Makk., i. p. 420, says the word means "those who try to imitate the Arabs in manners and language."

as heretofore.[1] In Cordova alone we find mention of the
following churches :[2] the Church of St Acislus, a former
martyr of Cordova; of St Zoilus; of the Three Martyrs
—Faustus, Januarius, Martialis; of St Cyprian; of SS.
Genesius and Eulalia; and of the Virgin Mary.

Of the last of these there is an interesting account in an
Arab writer, who died in 1034.[3] "I once entered at night,"
he says, "into the principal Christian Church. I found it
all strewed with green branches of myrtle, and planted with
cypress trees. The noise of the thundering bells resounded
in my ears; the glare of the innumerable lamps dazzled my
eyes; the priests, decked in rich silken robes of gay and
fanciful colours, and girt with girdle cords, advanced to
adore Jesus. Everyone of those present had banished
mirth from his countenance, and expelled from his mind
all agreeable ideas; and if they directed their steps towards
the marble font it was merely to take sips of water with the
hollow of their hands. The priest then rose and stood
among them, and taking the wine cup in his hands prepared
to consecrate it : he applied to the liquor his parched lips,
lips as dark as the dusky lips of a beautiful maid; the
fragrancy of its contents captivated his senses, but when he
had tasted the delicious liquor, the sweetness and flavour
seemed to overpower him." On leaving the church, the
Arab, with true Arabian facility, extemporized some verses
to the following effect: "By the Lord of mercy! this mansion of God is pervaded with the smell of unfermented red
liquor, so pleasant to the youth. It was to a girl that their
prayers were addressed, it was for her that they put on their

---

[1] Eulog., Letter to Alvar. After the death of Flora he says he spent
the ninth hour in prayer, then "auctis tripudiis, vespertinum, matutinum,
missale sacrificium consequenter ad honorem (Dei) et gloriam nostrarum
virginum celebravimus."

[2] Florez, x. 245.

[3] Ahmed ibn Abdilmalik ibn Shoheyd, Al Makk., i. 246. I quote
De Gayangos' translation.

gay tunics, instead of humiliating themselves before the Almighty." Ahmed also says : "the priests, wishing us to stay long among them, began to sing round us with their books in their hands ; every wretch presented us the palm of his withered hand (with the holy water), but they were even like the bat, whose safety consists in his hatred for light; offering us every attraction that their drinking of new wine, or their eating of swine's flesh, could afford." This narrative is in many respects very characteristic of an Arab writer, who would not feel the incongruity of an illustration on such a theme drawn from "the lips of a maid," or the irrelevancy of a reference to swine's flesh. But the account merits attention on other grounds, for it shews how little even the more intelligent Moslems understood the ceremonies of the religion which they had conquered, though they might be pardoned for thinking that the Christians worshipped the Virgin Mary, both because Mohammed himself fell into the same error, and because probably the Roman Church and its adherents had already begun to pay her idolatrous worship.

The chief church in Cordova at the conquest seems to have been the church of St Vincent. On the taking of the town,[1] the Christians had to give up half of it to the Arabs, a curious arrangement, but one enforced elsewhere by the Saracens. In 784 the Christians were induced, or compelled, to sell their half for 100,000 dinars, and it was pulled down to make room for the Great Mosque.[2] In 894 we find that the Cordovans were allowed to build a new church.

[1] De Gayangos on Al Makk., i. 368, says the cathedral was at first guaranteed to the Christians. Some time later than 750 they had to surrender half of it ; in 784 they were obliged to sell the other half, and in return were allowed to rebuild the destroyed churches. For the "church of the burnt" see above, p. 29, note 1.

[2] This was not finished till 793. The original structure cost 80,000 dinars. Several Khalifs added to it, and Hakem II. (961-976) alone spent on it 160,000 dinars.

Besides these within the walls, there were ten or twelve monasteries and churches in the immediate neighbourhood of Cordova : among them the monastery of St Christopher, the famous one of Tabanos, suppressed as above mentioned, in 854 ;[1] those of St Felix at Froniano, of St Martin at Royana, of the Virgin Mary at Cuteclara, of St Salvator at Pegnamellar; and the churches of SS. Justus and Pastor, and of St Sebastian.

We have given the names of these churches and monasteries[2] at or near Cordova, both to shew how numerous they were, and also because from one or other of them came nearly all the self-devoted martyrs, of whom we are about to consider the claims. Except in cases like that above-mentioned, the Christians were not allowed to build new churches,[3] but considering the diminution in the numbers of the Christians owing to the conquest, and the apostasy of a great many, this could not be reckoned a great hardship. Moreover the Christian churches, it was ordained, should be open to Moslems as well as Christians, though during the performance of mass it seems that they had to be kept closed. The Mosques were never to be polluted by the step of an infidel.[4]

The religious ferment, which manifested itself so strongly at Cordova, did not extend to other parts of Spain. For instance, at Elvira, the cradle of Spanish Christianity, it was shortly after the Cordovan martyrdoms (in 864) that the mosque, founded in the year of the conquest, and left

---

[1] Dozy, ii. 162.

[2] Monasteries were established in Spain 150 years before the Saracen conquest. They mostly fared badly at the hands of the Arabs, in spite of the injunctions of the Khalif Abubeker (see Conde, i. 37, and Gibbon), but that of Lorban at Coimbra received a favourable charter in 734 (Fleury, v. 89 ; but Dunham, ii. 154, doubts the authenticity of the charter).

[3] Cp. the stipulation of Omar at the fall of Jerusalem.

[4] See Charter of Coimbra, apud Fleury, v. 89.

unbuilt for 150 years, was finally finished. What we hear about the Christians at Elvira at this time is not to their credit, their bishop, Samuel, being notorious as an evil liver.[1] It is in Cordova that the main interest at this period centres; and to Cordova we will for the present confine our attention.

There is abundant evidence to shew that the party of enthusiasts, both those who offered themselves for martyrdom, and those who aided and abetted their more impulsive brethren, were a comparatively small body in the Church of Spain; and that their proceedings awakened little short of dismay in the minds of the more sensible portion of the Christian community, both in the Arab part of Spain, and perhaps in a less degree in the free North.[2] The chief leaders of the party of zealots—as far as we find mention of them—were Saul, bishop of Cordova (850-861), Eulogius, and Samson, abbot of the monastery of Pegnamellar; while Reccafredus, bishop of Seville, and Hostegesis of Malaga, were the prominent ecclesiastics on the other side.

Before relating what steps the latter took in conjunction with the Moslem authorities to put down the dangerous outbreak of fanaticism, it will be interesting to note what was the attitude of the different sections of the Church towards the misguided men who gave themselves up to death, and their claims to the crown of martyrdom. Those who denied the validity of these claims, rested their contention on the grounds, that the so-called martyrs had compassed their own destruction, there being no persecution at the time; that they had worked no miracles in proof of their high claims; that they had been slain by men who believed in the true God; that they had suffered an easy and immediate death; and that their bodies had corrupted like those of other men.

[1] Ibn Khatib, apud Dozy, ii. 210.   [2] Yonge, p. 63.

It was an abuse of words, said the party of moderation, to call these suicides by the holy name of martyrs, when no violence in high places had forced them to deny their faith,[1] or interfered with their due observance of Christianity.. It was merely an act of ostentatious pride—and pride was the root of all evil—to court danger. Such conduct had never been enjoined by Christ, and was quite alien from the meekness and humility of His character.[2]

They might have added that such voluntary martyrdoms had been expressly condemned,

(*a.*) By the circular letter of the Church of Smyrna to the other churches, describing Polycarp's martyrdom, in the terms : "We commend not those who offer themselves of their own accord, for that is not what the gospel teacheth us : "[3]

(*b.*) By St Cyprian,[4] who, when brought before the consul and questioned, said " our discipline forbiddeth that any should offer themselves of their own accord ; " and in his last letter he says : " Let none of you offer himself to the pagans, it is sufficient if he speak when apprehended : "

(*c.*) By Clement of Alexandria : " We also blame those who rush to death, for there are some, not of us, but only bearing the same name, who give themselves up : "[5]

(*d.*) Implicitly by the synod of Elvira, or Illiberis (*circa* 305), one of the canons of which forbade him to be

---

[1] Eul., "Mem. Sanct.," i., sec. 18, Quos nulla praesidalis violentia fidem suam negare compulit, nec a cultu sanctae piaeque religionis amovit:" sec. 23, "Quos liberalitas regis suum incolere iusserat Christianismum."

[2] Quoting such texts as Matt. v. 44, " Bless them that curse you, and pray for them that despitefully use you :" Pet. ii. 23, " Submit yourselves to every ordinance of man for the Lord's sake."

[3] Eusebius iv. 15. See Neander, i. p. 150. (A.D. 167.)

[4] Martyred 258.

[5] See Long's "M. Aurelius Antoninus," Introd., p. 21.

ranked as a martyr, who was killed on the spot for breaking idols:

(*e.*) By Mensurius, bishop of Carthage, who, when consulted on the question of reducing the immense lists of acknowledged martyrs, gave it as his opinion that those should be first excluded who had courted martyrdom.[1] One bishop alone, and he a late one, Benedict XIV. of Rome,[2] has ventured to approve what the Church has condemned. Nor is this the only instance in which the Roman Church has set aside the decisions of an earlier Christendom.

The charges against the zealots were twofold, that there had been no persecution worthy of the name, such as to justify their doings, and that those doings themselves were contrary to the teaching and spirit of Christianity. The latter part of the charge has already been dealt with, and may be considered sustained. As to the other part, the apologists, it must be confessed, answer with a very uncertain sound. Sometimes, indeed, they deny it pointblank:[3] "as if," says Eulogius, "the destruction of our churches,[4] the insults heaped upon our clergy, the monthly tax[5] which we pay, the perils of a hard life, lived on sufferance, are nothing." These insults and affronts are continually referred to. "No one," says the same author,[6] "can go out or come in amongst us in security, no one pass a knot of Moslems in the street without being treated with contumely. They mock at the marks[7] of our order. They hoot at us and call us fools and vain. The very children jeer at us, and even throw stones and potsherds at the

---

[1] Burton's "History of the Christian Church," p. 336.

[2] 1740-1748: in his "De Servorum Dei beatificatione et beatorum canonizatione," Bk. iii. 16, sec. 7. Fleury, v. 541.

[3] Eul., "Mem. Sanct.," i. sec. 21: Alvar, "Ind. Lum.," sec. 3.

[4] *Ibid.;* and Alvar, "Ind Lum.," sec. 7.

[5] Leovigild, "De habitu Clericorum." "Migne," 121, p. 565.

[6] Eul., l.l.   [7] Stigmata.

priests. The sound of the church-going bell[1] never fails to evoke from Moslem hearers the foulest and most blasphem-ous language. They even deem it a pollution to touch a Christian's garment." Alvar adds that the Moslems would fall to cursing when they saw the cross;[2] and when they witnessed a burial according to Christian rites, would say aloud, "Shew them no mercy, O God," throwing stones withal at the Lord's people, and defiling their ears with the filthiest abuse.[3] "Yet," he indignantly exclaims, "you say that this is not a time of persecution; nor is it, I answer, a time of apostles. But I affirm that it is a deadly time[4] . . . are we not bowed beneath the yoke of slavery, burdened with intolerable taxes, spoiled of our goods, lashed with the scourges of their abuse, made a byword and a proverb, aye, a spectacle to all nations?"[5]

That there was a certain amount of social ill-treatment, and that the lower classes of Moslems did not take any pains to conceal their dislike and scorn of such Christian beliefs and rites as were at variance with their own creed, and moreover regarded priests and monks with especial aversion, there can be no doubt. But, on the other hand,

---

[1] Alvar, "Ind. Lum.," sec. 6, "Derisioni et contemptui inhiantes capita moventes infanda iterando congeminant." He adds : "Daily and nightly from their minarets they revile the Lord by their invoca-tion of Allah and Mohammed!" Eul., "Lib. Ap.," sec. 19, confesses that hearing their call to prayer always moved him to quote Psalm xcvi. 7 : "Confounded be all they that worship carved images"—a very irrelevant malediction, as applied to the Moslems.

[2] Alvar, l.l., "Fidei signum opprobrioso elogio decolorant."

[3] "Spurcitiarum fimo."—*Ibid.*

[4] "Mortiferum."—"Ind. Lum.," sec. 3.

[5] Alvar, "Ind. Lum.," sec. 31, gives us a very savage picture of the Moslem character: "Sunt in superbia tumidi, in tumore cordis elati, in delectatione carnalium operum fluidi, in comestione superflui . . . sine misericordia crudeles, sine iustitia invasores, sine honore absque veritate, benignitatis nescientes affectum. . . . humilitatem velut in-saniam deridentes, castitatem velut spurcitiam respuentes."

there is no want of evidence to show that the condition of the Christians was by no means so bad as the apologists would have us suppose. Petty annoyances could not fail to exist anywhere under such circumstances, as were actually to be found in Spain at this time, and we may be sure that the Christian priests in particular did not bear themselves with that humility which might have ensured a mitigation of the annoyances. Organised opposition to Christianity, unless the Moslem rule can itself be called such, there was none, till it was called into being by the action of the fanatics themselves. But apart from all the other facts which point to this conclusion, we can call the apologists themselves in evidence that there was no real persecution going on at the time of the first martyrdoms.

Eulogius [1] admits that the Christians were not let or hindered in the free exercise of their religion by saying that this state of things [2] was not due to the forbearance (forsooth!) of the Moslems, but to the Divine mercy. Alvar, too, in a passage which seems to contradict the whole position which he is trying to defend, says [3] :—" Though many were the victims of persecution, very many others—and you cannot deny it—offered themselves a voluntary sacrifice to the Lord. Is it not clear that it was not the Arabs who began persecuting, but we who began preaching? Read the story of the martyrs, and you will see that they rushed voluntarily on their fate, not waiting the bidding of persecutors, nor the snares of informers; aye, and—what is made so strong a charge against them—that they tired out the forbearance of their rulers and princes by insult upon insult." [4]

As to the other part of the accusation, that voluntary

---

[1] " Mem. Sanct.," i. sec. 29.
[2] Viz., " Quod inter ipsos sine molestia fidei degimus."
[3] " Ind. Lum.," sec. 3.
[4] " Fatigasse praesides et principes multis contumeliis."—*Ibid.*

martyrs were no martyrs, Eulogius could only declaim against the Scriptures quoted by his opponents,[1] and refer to the morally blind, who make evil their good, and take darkness to be their light;[2] while he brought forward a saying of certain wise men that "those martyrs will hold the first rank in the heavenly companies who have gone to their death unsummoned."[3]

He also sought to defend the practice of reviling Mohammed by the plea that exorcism was allowed against the devil, which is sufficiently ridiculous; but Alvar goes further, and calmly assures us that these insults and revilings of the prophet were merely a form of preaching[4] to the poor benighted Moslems, naïvely remarking that the Scriptures affirm that the Gospel of Christ must be preached to all nations. Whereas, then, the Moslems had not been preached to, these martyred saints had taken upon themselves the sacred duty of rendering them "debtors to the faith."

The second count[5] against the martyrs was that they had worked no miracles—a serious deficiency in an age when miracles were almost the test of sanctity. Eulogius[6] could only meet the charge by admitting the fact, but adding that miracles were frequent in the early ages, in order to establish Christianity on a firm basis; and that the constancy of the martyrs was in itself a miracle (which was true, but not to the point). Had he been content with this, he had done wisely; but he goes on: " Moreover, miracles are

---

[1] Eul., "Mem. Sanct.," i. sec. 19.   [2] Isaiah v. 20.

[3] Eul., "Mem. Sanct.," i. sec. 24. Taken from some "Acts of the Saints," probably those of SS. Emetherius and Caledonius—a book obviously of no authority.

[4] "Ind. Lum.," sec. 10, "In hac Israelitica gente nullus hactenus exstitit praedicator, per quod debitores fidei tenerentur. Isti enim (*i.e.*, the martyrs) apostolatus vicem in eosdem et evangelicam praedicationem impleverunt, eosque fidei debitores reddiderunt."

[5] Eul., "Mem. Sanct.," i. 13.   [6] "Lib. Apol.," sec 7.

no sign of truth, as even the unbelievers can work them." [1]
Now, by trying to show why these martyrs did not perform
any miracles, he admits by implication that they were de-
ficient in this particular ; [2] and yet in other parts of his
work he mentions miracles performed by these very martyrs,
as, for instance, by Isaac, and by Flora, and Maria. [3]   So that
the worthy priest is placed in this dilemma : If miracles are
really no sign of truth, why attribute them to the martyrs,
when, as is allowed elsewhere, they were unable to work
them ? if, on the other hand, they did perform these miracles,
why not adduce them in evidence against the detractors ?

The third objection is a curious one, that the martyrs
were not put to death by idolaters, but by men worshipping
God and acknowledging a divine law, [4] and therefore were
not true martyrs.   Eulogius misses the true answer, which
is obvious enough, and scornfully exclaims :—"As if they
could be said to believe in God, who persecute His Church,
and deem it hateful to believe in a Christ who was very
God and very man." [5]

Fourthly, the martyrs died a quick and easy death.   But,
as Eulogius points out, [6] pain and torture give no additional
claim to the martyr's crown.

Lastly, it was objected that the bodies of these martyrs,
as indeed was to be expected, corrupted, and were even,
in some cases, devoured by dogs.   "What matter," says
Eulogius, [7] "since their souls are borne away to celestial
mansions."

But it was not objections brought by fellow-Christians
only that Eulogius took upon himself to answer, but also
the taunts and scoffs of the Moslems.   "Why," said they,
"if your God is the true God, does He not strike terror into

---

[1] " Lib. Apol.," sec. 10.   [2] Cp. "Mem. Sanct.," i. sec. 13.
[3] "Mem. Sanct.," Pref., sec. 4.
[4] Eul. "Lib. Apol.," sec. 3.   [5] *Ibid.*, sec. 12.
[6] *Ibid.*, sec. 5.   [7] "Mem. Sanct.," i. sec. 17.

the executioners of his saints by some great prodigy? and why do not the martyrs themselves flash forth into miracles while the crowd is round them? You rush upon your own destruction, and yet you work no wonders that might induce us to change our opinion of your creed, thereby doing your own side no good, and ours no harm." [1]

Yet the constancy of the martyrs affected the Moslems more than they cared to confess, as we may infer from the taunts levelled at the Christians, when, in Mohammed's reign, some Christians, from fear of death, even apostatized. " Whither," they triumphantly asked, [2] " has that bravery of your martyrs vanished? What has become of the rash frenzy with which they courted death?" Yet though they affected to consider the martyrs as fools or madmen, they could not be blind to the effect that their constancy was likely to produce on those who beheld their death, and to the reverence with which their relics were regarded by the Christians. They therefore expressly forbade the bodies of martyrs to be preserved [3] and worshipped, and did their best to make this in certain cases impossible by burning the corpses and scattering the ashes on the river, though sometimes they contented themselves with throwing the bodies, unburnt, into the stream.

However, in spite of these regulations, many bodies were secretly carried off and entombed in churches, where they

---

[1] "Mem. Sanct.," i. sec. 12.

[2] Eulog., "Mem. Sanct.," iii. sec. 6.

[3] See "De Translatione corporum Sanctorum Martyrum," etc., sec. 11. "Non enim, quos martyres faciunt, venerari Saraceni permittunt." See above, p. 38. The bodies of earlier martyrs were more freely given up at the request of the Christians. See "Chron. Silen.," secs. 95-100; Dozy, iv. 119, for the surrender of the body of Justus; and Eul., "Ad Wiliesindum," sec. 9, where Eulogius mentions that he had taken the bodies of Saints Zoilus and Austus to Pampluna. Later, Hakem II. (961-976) gave up the body of the boy Pelagius at Ramiro III.'s request. Mariana, viii. 5.

E

were looked upon as the most precious of possessions; and martyrs, who, by the admission of their admirers themselves, had never worked any miracles when living, were enabled, when dead, to perform a series of extraordinary ones, which did not finally cease till modern enlightenment had dissipated the darkness of the Middle Ages.

We happen to possess a very interesting account of the circumstances under which the relics of three of these Cordovan martyrs were transferred from the troubled scene of their passion to the more peaceful and more superstitious cloisters of France.[1]

It was in 858 that Hilduin, the abbot of the monastery of St Vincent and the Holy Cross, near Paris, learning that the body of their patron saint, St Vincent, was at Valencia, sent two monks, Usuard and Odilard, with the king's[2] permission, to procure the precious relics for their own monastery. On their way to perform this commission, the monks learnt that the body was no longer at Valencia. It had been, in fact, carried[3] by a monk named Andaldus to Saragoza. Senior, the bishop of that city, had seized it, and it was still held in veneration there, but under the name of St Marinus, whose body the monk had stoutly asserted it to be. Senior apparently doubted the statement, and tortured Andaldus to get the truth out of him, but in vain; for the monk, knowing that St Vincent had been deacon of Saragoza, feared that the bishop would never surrender the body if aware of its identity. However, Usuard and Odilard knew not but that the body was that of Marinus, as stated.

Disappointed, therefore, in their errand, they lingered about at Barcelona, thinking to pick up some other relics, when a friend, holding a high position in that town, Sunifridus by name, mentioned the persecution at Cordova, news

---

[1] De Translatione SS. martyrum Georgii, Aurelii, et Nathaliae ex urbe Cordobae Parisios : auctore Aimoino.—"Migne," vol. 115, pp. 939 ff.

[2] Charles the Bald.   [3] "Under a divine impulse," as usual.

of which does not seem to have travelled beyond Spain. They determine at once to go to Cordova, relying on a friend there, named Leovigild, to help them to obtain what they wished. Travelling in Spain, however, seems to have been by no means safe[1] at this period, and their bold resolution is regarded with fear and admiration by their friends. The lord of the Gothic marches, Hunifrid, being on friendly terms with the Wali of Saragoza, writes to him on their behalf, and he entrusts them to the care of a caravan which chanced to be just starting for Cordova.

On reaching Cordova, after many days, they go to St Cyprian's Church, where lay the bodies of John and Adulphus. The rumour of their arrival brings Leovigild (called Abad Salomes), who proves a very useful friend, and Samson, who just at this juncture is made abbot of the monastery at Pegnamellar, where the bodies of George, Aurelius, and Sabigotha were buried—the very relics which they had decided to try and obtain.

The monks of the monastery naturally object to parting with such precious possessions, but Samson contrives to get the bishop's permission to give up the bodies.

This was all the more opportune, as a chance was now given them of returning to Barcelona, by joining the expedition which Mohammed I. was on the point of making against Toledo. Orders had been given that all the inhabitants, strangers as well as citizens, except the city guard, should go out with the King. However, the Frankish monks were met by an unexpected difficulty. In the temporary absence of the abbot, the monks of Pegnamellar refused to give up the relics, and it was only with much difficulty that the bishop Saul was induced to confirm his former permission to remove them.

[1] See sec. 2, and Eul., "Ad Wiliesindum," where he speaks of the road to Gaul as "stipata praedonibus," and of all Gothia as "perturbata funeroso Wilihelmi incursu."

The bodies were now exhumed without the knowledge of the Moslems, and sealed with Charles' own seal, brought for that purpose. George's body was found whole, but of the other two, only the head of Nathalia, and the trunk of Aurelius' body. The two latter are united to form one corpse, as it is written, "they two shall be one flesh." After a stay in Cordova of eight weeks, they set out under the protection of some Christians serving in the army. Leovigild, who had been away on the King's business, now returns, and escorts them to Toledo. The approach of the army having cleared away the brigands who infested those parts, the monks with their precious freight got safely away to Saragoza, and returned with their booty to France, where the relics worked numbers of astonishing miracles.

Let us return from this digression to the steps taken by the moderate party among the Christians, and by the Moslem authorities, to put an end to what seemed so dangerous an agitation. That Reccafredus was not the only ecclesiastic of high position who took exception to the new movement we learn clearly enough from Alvar,[1] who tells us that "bishops, priests, deacons, and 'wise men' of Cordova joined in inveighing against the new martyrdoms, under the impulse of fear wellnigh denying the faith of Christ, if not in words, yet by their acts." We may, therefore, conclude that the greater part of the ecclesiastical authorities were heart and soul with the Bishop of Seville, while the party led by Eulogius and Saul was a comparatively small one. However, strong measures were necessary, and Reccafredus did not hesitate to imprison several priests and clergy.[2] Eulogius complains that the churches were

---

[1] "Life of Eulog.," ch. i. sec. 4.

[2] Alvar, "Life of Eulog.," ii. sec. 4—"Omnes sacerdotes quos potuit carcerali vinculo alligavit." Eul., "Doc. Martyr," sec. 11— "Repleta sunt penetralia carceris clericorum catervis, viduata est ecclesia

deprived of their ministers, and the customary church rites were in abeyance, "while the spider wove her web in the deserted aisles, tenanted only by a dreadful silence." In this passage the writer doubtless gives reins to his imagination, yet there must have been a certain amount of truth in the main assertion, for he repeats it again and again.[1]

The evidence of Alvar is to the same effect : "Have not those who seemed to be columns of the church, the very rocks on which it is founded, who were deemed the elect of God, have they not, I say, in the presence of these Cynics, or rather of these Epicureans, under no compulsion, but of their own free will, spoken evil of the martyrs of God? Have not the shepherds of Christ, the teachers of the Church, bishops, abbots, priests, the chiefs of our hierarchy, and its mighty men, publicly denounced the martyrs of our Church as heretics?"[2]

Not content with imprisoning the fanatics, the party of order forced them to swear that they would not snatch at the martyr's palm by speaking evil of the Prophet.[3] Those who disobeyed were threatened with unheard-of penalties, with loss of limbs, and merciless scourgings.[4] This last statement must be taken with reservation, at least if put into the mouth of the Christian party under Reccafredus.

sacro praesulum et sacerdotum officio . . . privata prorsus ecclesia omni sacro ministerio." Alvar, "Ind. Lum.," secs. 14, 18—"Templa Christi a sacrificio desolata, et loca sancta ab ethnicis exstirpata."

[1] Eul., "Doc. Mart.," sec. 16—"Eremitatem ecclesiarum, compeditionem sacerdotum . . . et quod non est nobis in hoc tempore sacrificium nec holocaustum nec oblatio." Cp. Ep. ad Wilies, sec. 10.

[2] Alvar, "Ind. Lum.," sec. 14.

[3] *Ibid.*, sec. 15—"Ne ad martyrii surgerent palmam, iuramentum extorsimus . . . et maledictum ne maledictionibus impeterent, evangelio et cruce educta, vi iurare improbiter fecimus."

[4] *Ibid.*, cp. Alvar, "Life of Eulog.," iv. sec. 12—"Duris tormentis agitati, commoti sunt."

It is extremely unlikely that Christian bishops and priests should have had recourse to such treatment of their co-religionists: yet they had a spiritual weapon ready to their hands, and they were not slow to use it. They anathematised[1] those who aided and abetted the zealots; and Eulogius himself seems to have narrowly escaped their sentence of excommunication.[2]

This action against the zealots was in all probability taken, if not at the instigation of the Moslem authorities, yet in close concert with them. Eulogius[3] attributes all the evils which had befallen the Church, such as the imprisonment of bishops, priests, abbots, and deacons, to the wrath of the King; and Alvar distinctly states that the King was urged, even bribed, to take measures against the Christians.[4] It is not likely that the King required much persuading. Mohammed at least seems to have been thoroughly frightened by the continued agitation against Mohammedanism. He naturally suspected some political plot at the bottom of it; a supposition which receives some countenance from the various references in Eulogius[5] to the martyrs as "Soldiers of God" bound to war against His Moslem enemies; and from the undoubted fact that the Christians of Toledo did rise in favour of their coreligionists at Cordova.[6] However that may be, the King in 852 certainly took counsel[7] with his ministers, how the agitation should be met, and he seems to have

---

[1] Eulog., "Mem. Sanct.," i. sec. 28—"Ne ceteri ad huiusmodi palaestram discurrant schedulis anathematum per loca varia damnari iubentur." Alvar, "Ind. Lum.," sec. 31—"Plerosque patres anathematizantes talia patientes."

[2] Eulog., "Mem. Sanct.," iii. c. iv. sec. 5.

[3] Ep. ad Wilies, sec. 10.

[4] Alvar, "Ind. Lum.," sec. 35.   [5] See Dozy, ii. 136.

[6] Conde, i. 249: Dozy, ii. 161, says on Eulogius' authority, that he incited them to revolt under Sindila.

[7] Eulog., "Mem. Sanct.," ii. c. xiv.

assembled a sort of grand council[1] of the Church, when the same question was discussed. Stronger measures were in consequence taken, and a more rigorous imprisonment resorted to. But Mohammed went farther than this. He deprived of their posts all Christians, who held offices in the palace,[2] or in connection with the Court, and withdrew from the Christian "cadet corps,"[3] the royal bounty usually extended to them. He ordered the destruction of all churches built since the conquest, and of all later additions to those previously existing. He made a severe enactment against those who reviled Mohammed.[4] He even had in mind to banish all Christians from his dominions.[5] This intention, together with the order respecting the churches, was not carried out, owing probably to the opportune revolt at Toledo.[6]

In one of his works on this subject, Eulogius expresses a fear lest the intervention of the martyrs should bring disaster on the Church in Spain, just as the intervention of Moses in Egypt did much at first to aggravate the hardships of the Israelites.[7] He ought not, therefore, to have been surprised, when such a result actually did follow; nor ought he to complain that now the Moslems would only let the Christians observe their religion in such a way as they chose to dictate; and that the

[1] Robertson calls it a Conciliabulum.

[2] Eulog., "Mem. Sanct.," ii. § 2.

[3] " Militares pueros." Eulog. "Mem. Sanct.," iii. c. i.

[4] Eulog. "Mem. Sanct.," ii. c. xiv.—"Tunc iam procul dubio enecandi nos difficultas fuit adempta, si quisquam vatis sui temerarius exprobator ultro occurreret." This seems to mean that Christians and Saracens were bound to give up to justice any who reviled the Prophet ; or else to kill him on the spot.

[5] Eulog., "Doc. Mart.," sec. 18—"Moslemi . . . omne regni sui, sicuti cernitis, genus excludere moliuntur Christicolarum."

[6] Eulog., "Mem. Sanct.," iii. c. iv.

[7] *Ibid.,* ii. c. xvi.

Christians were subjected to all sorts of taxes and exactions.[1]

These combined measures of repression, taken by the King and the Bishop of Seville, soon produced their effect. The extreme party were broken up, some escaping to quieter regions, others hiding, and only venturing abroad in disguise and at night—not, as Eulogius is careful to add, from fear of death, but because the high prize of martyrdom is not reserved for the unworthy many, but for the worthy few.[2]

Some even apostatized,[3] while many of those who had applauded the proceedings of the martyrs, now called them indiscreet, and blamed them for indulging in a selfish desire to desert the suffering Church for an early mansion in the skies.[4] Others, in order to retain posts under Government, or to court favour with the King, dissembled their religion, taking care not to pray, or make the sign of the cross in public.[5] Eulogius himself was singled out at the meeting of the King's Council by one of the royal secretaries, Gomez, son of Antonian, son of Julian,[6] as the

[1] Eulog., "Doc. Mart.," sec. 18—"*Nunc* pro suo libito tantummodo exercere nos sinentes Christianismum . . . *nunc* publicum imponentes censum, *nunc* rebus nos abdicantes detrimentis atterunt rerum."

[2] Eulog., "Mem. Sanct.," ii. sec. 14—"Quia indigni sumus martyrio, quod quibusdam et non omnibus datum est."

[3] Eulog., "Mem. Sanct.," ii. c. xv. 1—"Fidem praevaricantur, abdicant religionem, Crucifixum detestantur."

[4] Eulog., "Mem. Sanct.," ii. c. ii. sec. 6. Also in his letter to Alvar sending the "Mem. Sanct.," he says, very few remained firm to their principles.

[5] Alvar, "Ind. Lum.," sec. 9—"Cum palam coram ethnicis orationem non faciunt, signo crucis oscitantes frontem non muniunt. . . . Christianos contra fidei suae socios pro regis gratia, pro vendibilibus muneribus et defensione gentilicia praeliantes." Elsewhere he says: "Nullus invenitur qui iuxta iussum Domini tonantis aetherii super montes Babiloniae, caligosasque turres crucis fidei attollat vexillum, sacrificium Deo offerens vespertinum."

[6] Eulog., "Mem. Sanct.," iii. c. iv. sec. 5: Alvar, "Ind. Lum.," sec. 18. See above, p. 51.

ringleader of the new seditious movement. This man was a very worldly-minded Christian,[1] and was, no doubt, at this time, in fear of losing his lucrative office at Court, which he had obtained by his remarkable knowledge of Arabic. He did, in fact, lose his post with all the other Christian officers of the Court, but regained it by becoming a Moslem ;[2] and such was the ardour of the new proselyte that he was called "the dove of the mosque."[3]

The result of this council was, as we have seen, hostile to the party of which Eulogius and Saul were the chiefs, but the former writer, mentioning the actual decree that was passed, pretends that it was merely a blind to deceive the king, and spoken figuratively ; and he acknowledges that such hypocrisy was unworthy of the prelates and officers assembled.[4] Is it not more reasonable to suppose that Eulogius and his supporters voted for it—as they seem to have done—with a mental reservation, while their opponents honestly considered such a step necessary ?

———o———

CHAPTER VI.

THE MUZARABES.

THE death of Eulogius was a signal for the cessation of the dubious martyrdoms which had for some years become so common, though the spirit, which prompted the self-deluded victims, was by no means stifled either in Spain

---

[1] Ibn al Kuttiya—apud Dozy, ii. 137.
[2] Eulog., " Mem. Sanct.," iii. c. ii.   [3] Dozy, ii. 137.
[4] Eul., "Mem. Sanct.," ii. c. xv., sec. 3—"Aliquid commentaremur, quod ipsius tyranni ac populorum serperet aures." The " praemissum pontificale decretum " he calls "allegorice editum."

or the adjoining countries.[1]   Yet the measures taken to put down the mania for death succeeded in preventing any fresh outbreak for some time.

Under the weak government of Abdallah (888-912) the Christians, determining to lose their lives to better purpose than at the hands of the executioner, rose in revolt, as will be related hereafter, in several parts of Spain.   After the battle of Aguilar, or Polei, in 891, between the Arab and Spanish factions, 1000 of the defeated Christians were given the choice of Islam or death, and all, save one, chose the latter alternative.[2]

During the long reign of Abdurrahman III. (912-961) there were a few isolated cases of martyrdom, which may as well be mentioned now.   After the great battle in the Vale of Rushes,[3] where Abdurrahman defeated the kings of Navarre and Leon, one of the two fighting bishops, who were taken prisoners on that occasion, gave, as a hostage for his own release, a youth of fourteen, named Pelagius. The king, it is said, smitten with his beauty, wished to work his abominable will upon the boy, but his advances being rejected with disdain, the unhappy youth was put to death with great barbarity, refusing to save his life by apostasy.[4] A different version of the story is given by a Saxon nun of Gaudersheim, named Hroswitha, who wrote a poem on the subject fifty years later.   She tells us that the king tried to kiss Pelagius, who thereupon struck him in the face, and was in consequence put to death by decapitation (June 26, 925).[5]

---

[1] See " Life of Argentea," secs. 3, 5.   [2] Dozy, ii. 287.

[3] Val du Junqueras, 920 A.D.

[4] Johannes Vasaeus ex Commentariis Resendi. Romey, iv. 257, disbelieves this version of the story.   Perhaps Al Makk., ii. 154, is referring to the same Pelagius when he mentions the king's liking for a handsome Christian page.

[5] Sampiro, secs. 26-28.

In the death of Argentea (Ap. 28, 931) we have the last instance in Spain of a Christian seeking martyrdom. She was the daughter of the great rebel Omar ibn Hafsun,[1] and his wife Columba, and was born at that chieftain's stronghold of Bobastro. Upon her mother's death Omar wished her to take up her mother's duties in the palace, for Omar had become a sort of king on his own domain. She declined, asking only for a quiet retreat, where she might prepare her soul for martyrdom; and she wrote to a devout Christian, whose wishes inclined him in the same direction, suggesting that they should seek the crown of martyrdom together.[2] On the destruction of Bobastro by Abdurrahman in 928, she went to Cordova.[3] She there met with a Gaul named Vulfura, who had been warned in a dream that in that city he should find a virgin, with whom he was to suffer martyrdom. However, his object becoming known, Vulfura is cast into prison by the governor of the city. Argentea goes to visit him there, and is stopped by the guards, who, finding she is a Christian, take her before the judge as a renegade, and she is imprisoned with Vulfura. The alternative of Islam instead of death being refused, they are both executed, but Argentea, as being an " insolens rebellis," is first scourged with 1000 stripes, and her tongue cut out. Her body was buried at the church of the three saints.

In the year 934 [4] we hear of two hundred monks of Cardena being massacred by the Berbers in Abdurrahman's army; and in some sense they can be regarded as martyrs to their faith.

---

[1] Who on becoming a Christian, took the name of Samuel. Florez, x. p. 564, ff.

[2] See " Life of Argentea," by an anonymous author.

[3] *Ibid.*, sec. 4.

[4] Dozy, iii. 52. Mariana, viii. 6, gives 993, but says it may have occurred in 893.

In 953 a martyr named Eugenia is said to have perished; [1] and thirty years later, the last martyrs of whom we have any record under the Arab rule. Dominicus Sarracinus, son of John, and his companions taken prisoners at the capture of Simancas, were kept for two years and a-half in prison.[2] They were then brought out and put to death, just when Ramiro III., or his successor, had sent to ransom them.[3]

There is no evidence whatever to show that there was a persecution of the Christians under the great Abdurrahman, and the statements of those writers who intimate the contrary may be set aside as unsupported by evidence.[4]

We will now turn back and take a general view of the Christian Church and its condition under the Arabs in Spain, especially—for our information is greatest as to those periods—under the two kings Abdurrahman II. and III.

Under the former of these sovereigns the condition of the Christians, until the persecution, which they themselves provoked, began, was very tolerable, and the majority of the Christians were quite content with their lot. They served in the army, both free men and slaves; they held lucrative posts at Court, or in the houses of the Arab nobles, or as government officials. But though the lay community was well off, the clergy and stricter churchmen had something to complain of; for the Church [5] could not be said to be free, though the worship was, since the power of summoning councils had now passed to the Arab executive, who, as we have seen, made even Moslems and Jews sit at these councils. Sees were also put up to auction, and the scandalous spectacle was not unknown, of atheists and

---

[1] Schott., iv. 246.   [2] Rohrbacher, xii. 192.

[3] Charter, apud Florez, xiv. 397.

[4] See above, p. 36, note 1. A letter also is mentioned of John Servus Dei, Bishop of Toledo, to the Muzarabes with regard to the late martyrdoms and apostasies, purporting to have been written in 937.

[5] Dozy, ii. 47.

heretics holding the titles, and drawing the emoluments, of bishops.[1]

As was to be expected, Arabic soon began to displace Latin throughout the country, and even before the ninth century the Scriptures were translated into the tongue of the conquerors [2] by Odoarius, Bishop of Accita, and John of Seville. Hischem I. (788-796) forbade the use of any language but Arabic, so that his Christian subjects had to use Arabic Gospels;[3] and the Spaniards were soon not even permitted to write in Latin.[4] Even if this statement be doubtful, we know that Latin came gradually to be neglected and forgotten. Alvar utters an eloquent protest against this : "Alas, the Christians are ignorant of their own tongue, and Latins neglect their language, so that in all the College of Christ [5] there is scarcely to be found one who can write an address of welcome to his brother intelligibly in Latin, while numbers can be found competent to mouth the flowery rhetoric of the Chaldeans." [6] In the department of poetry—the peculiar boast of the Arabs—the Christians seem even to have surpassed their masters ; and to the rivalry of the two nations in this art we may attribute the excellence and abundance of native ballads of which Spain can boast.

We have seen how Eulogius did his best to check this neglect of Latin, by introducing into Spain some of the masterpieces in that language; but it is doubtful whether his efforts had much result. We can see from the remains of the Spanish writers which we possess that the structure of that language had considerably degenerated in Spain.[7]

[1] Alvar, "Ep.," xiii. 3. Samson, "Apol.," ii. cc. ii.-iv.

[2] Murphy, "Hist. Mahom. Empire in Spain," p. 309.

[3] Yonge, p. 60.   [4] Conde, i. 239.

[5] "Omni Christi collegio."   [6] Alvar, "Ind. Lum.," sec. 35.

[7] See Elipandus and Alvar passim. Alcuin, on the other hand, writes wonderfully good Latin.

Some sentences are so ungrammatical as to be scarcely intelligible. Moreover, we find Samson [1] directly accusing Hostegesis, Bishop of Malaga, of not being able to write Latin; and similarly Jonas of Orleans (839) accusing Claudius, Bishop of Turin, who was himself a Spaniard, of the same defect.

The neglect of Latin was accompanied by an increasing indifference to the doctrinal basis of Christianity, educated Christians being led to devote their time, which might have been more profitably spent on their own Scriptures, to becoming acquainted with the Mohammedan religion, and even to unravelling the intricacies of the controversial theology which had grown up round, and overlaid, the original simplicity of the Koran.[2] The great Fathers of the Church were laid aside unread, and even the Prophets and Apostles, and the Gospel itself, found few to study them. While the higher classes were indifferent to religion, the lower were sunk in poverty [3] and ignorance.[4] The inevitable result of this indifference, ignorance, and poverty, was a visible deterioration in the character of Spanish Christianity, of which there are only too many proofs.

We find the abbot Samson distinctly accusing Hostegesis, Bishop of Malaga, of simony, asserting that he sold the

[1] Samson, "Apol.," c. vii.

[2] Alvar, "Ind. Lum.," sec. 35—"Ac dum illorum sacramenta in-quirimus, et philosophorum sectas scire non pro ipsorum convincendis erroribus sed pro elegantia leporis et locutione luculenter diserta. Quis rogo hodie solers in nostris fidelibus laicis invenitur, qui Scripturis sanctis intentus volumina quorumcunque Doctorum Latine conscripta respiciat? Quis Evangelico, quis Prophetico, quis Apostolico ustus tenetur amore? Nonne omnes iuvenes Christiani vultu decori, linguae diserti, habitu gestuque conspicui, Gentilicia eruditione praeclari, Arabico eloquio sublimati, volumina Chaldaeorum avidissime tractunt?"

[3] Florez, xix. 383, Charter of 993; see also "Dozy," iii. 31; and for the condition of Christians in the Free States, Buckle, "Hist. of Civiliz.," i. 443.
[4] Dozy (l.l.).

priesthood to low and unworthy people;[1] while Alvar charges Saul, Bishop of Cordova, with obtaining his bishopric by bribery.[2]   Other irregularities imputed to Hostegesis were that he held his see from his twentieth year, contrary to the canons of the church, and that he beat priests, in order to extort money from them, till they died under his hands.

Besides the election to the priesthood, by unworthy means, of unworthy men, whose ignorance and impudence the congregation had to endure in silence,[3] many were informally ordained without vouchers for character being given, or the assent of their fellow-clergy and flocks being obtained.[4]   Many churches presented the unseemly spectacle of two rival pastors, contrary to the ordinances received from the Fathers.[5]

Changes, too, were made in doctrine and ritual, for which no authority could be alleged, in contravention of established custom and the teaching of the Church.   So far was this carried that Samson was accused by his opponents of being a heretic and an idolator because he permitted the marriage of cousins; dissented from the view that God was ever enclosed in the chambers of the Virgin's heart;[6] asserted the omnipresence of God, even in idols and the Devil, and this in an actual, not a metaphysical, sense;[7] and denied

---

[1] Samson, "Apol.," Bk. ii., Pref. sec. 2.

[2] See "Letter to Saul," sec. 3—"Poterant enim quovis asserente canonice incohationis vestrae primordia comprobari, si quadringenti solidi non fuissent palam eunuchis vel aliis exsoluti." Dozy, ii. 140, adds that the money was guaranteed on the episcopal revenues, but this is a conjecture.

[3] Samson, "Apol.," ii. Pref. sec 5 ; Dozy, ii. 268.

[4] Alvar ad Saulum, sec. 3—"Sine testimonis, sine connibentia clericorum."   [5] *Ibid.*

[6] Samson, "Apol.," ii. Pref. sec. 7 and iii.—"Cubiculum cordis Virginei." This appears to be a quotation from the Gothic liturgy.

[7] "Per substantiam, non per subtilitatem."—*Ibid.*

that God sat upon an exalted throne above his creatures.
From this it is clear that Hostegesis and those who
thought with him[1] were infected with the anthropomorphite
heresy.

Not only did many of the clergy hold heretical views, but
their depravity was notorious.   Hostegesis did not blush to
spend the produce of the church tithes and offerings, which
he had with difficulty extorted from his flock,[2] in bribing the
court officials and the king's sons, giving them feasts at
which open and flagrant vice was indulged in.[3]   The clergy
were not above pretending illness in order to avoid paying
the monthly tax to their Moslem rulers.[4]   Some, even in
the highest positions in the Church, denied their Saviour
and apostatized to the Moslems ; one of these renegades
being Samuel, Bishop of Elvira, the uncle of Hostegesis'
mother, who, with a pervert's zeal, persecuted the Church
he had deserted, imprisoning the clergy, taxing his former
flock, and even forcing some to embrace Islam.[5]

It is not surprising, therefore, that bishops and clergy
were sometimes deposed.   Samson, indeed, underwent this
disgrace at the hands of a hostile faction under Hostegesis,
on the ground of his pretended heresy ; and, similarly,
Valentius,[6] Bishop of Cordova, was deprived of his see
because he was a supporter of Samson.   But these instances
reflect more discredit on the deposers than on their victims.
Instances of deposition are not wanting in the free states
the North.   Sisenandus, seventh Bishop of Compostella

---

[1] Romanus and Sebastianus, Samson, Pref, sec. 6.

[2] The offering of one-third for the Church was refused to Hostegesis
as being sacrilegious ; so he proceeded to extort it, "suis codicibus
institutis."—Samson "Apol.," ii. Pref. sec. 2.

[3] *Ibid.*   The state of the Church in the North was not much better.
See Yonge, p. 86.

[4] Leovigild de habitu Clericorum.   Dozy, ii. 110.

[5] Samson, Pref. ii. 4.

[6] Succeeded Saul in 861, and was deposed in 864.

(940), was deposed by King Sancho for dissolute living, and malversation of Church moneys.[1] On the king's death he recovered his see, driving out his successor. Pelayo, another bishop of Compostella, suffered the same punishment.[2]

When the kings of Castile gradually drove back the Moors, and when Alfonso took Toledo in 1085, his wife, Constance of Burgundy, and her spiritual adviser, a monk named Bernard, were horrified at the laxity in morals and doctrine of the Muzarabic Christians. Their addiction to poetry and natural science was regarded with suspicious aversion, and the pork-eating, circumcision, and, not least, the cleanly habits,[3] contracted from an intercourse with Moslems, were looked upon as so many marks of the beast. In 1209 the Crusaders, who had swarmed to the wars in Spain, even wished to turn their pious arms against these poor Muzarabes, so scandalised were they at the un-Romish rites. Yet we are told that Alfonso the Great, when building and restoring churches in the territory newly wrested from the Moors, set up again the ordinances of the Goths, as formerly observed at Toledo.[4]

The free church in the North had itself been in great danger of extinction, when the armies of the great Almanzer (977-1002) swept yearly through the Christian kingdoms like some devastating tempest.[5] Fifty-two victorious campaigns

---

[1] Mariana, viii. 5. He went over to the Moslems. Southey, "Chronicle of the Cid," p. 228. Yonge, p. 86.

[2] Mariana (l. l.).

[3] The Christians in the North were vulgarly supposed by the Arabs not to wash. See Conde, i. 203—"It is related of these people of Galicia . . . that they live like savages or wild beasts, and never wash either their persons or their garments."

[4] "Chron. Albeld.," sec. 58—"Ordinem Gothorum sicuti Toleto fuerat statuit."

[5] "Chron. Silense," sec. 72—"Eadem tempestate in Hispania omnis divinus cultus periit."

F

did that irresistible warrior lead against the infidels.[1]   Barcelona, Pampluna, and Leon fell before his arms, and the sacred city of Compostella was sacked, and for a time left desolate, the bells of St James' shrine being carried off to Cordova to serve as lamps in the grand mosque. We are not, therefore, surprised to find that there were many bishops in the North who had lost their sees ; and this was the case even before the tenth century, for a bishop named Sabaricus, being driven from his own see by the Arabs, was given that of Mindumetum by Alfonso III. in 867,[2] and twenty years later a bishop named Sebastian received the see of Auria in the same way.[3]

It is natural enough that the Moslems and the clergy of the Christian Church should be hostile to one another, but it is surprising to find—as we do find in some cases —the latter making common cause with the Arabs in ill-treating their fellow-countrymen and coreligionists. Thus, as we have seen, Hostegesis, relying on the support of the secular arm,[4] beat and imprisoned the clergy for withholding from him the Church tithes, dragging them through the city naked, with a crier crying before them :—"Such is the punishment of those who will not pay their tithes to their bishop."[5]   Bishops were even found to make episcopal visitations, getting the names of all their flock, as if with the intention of praying for them individually, and then to hand in their names to the civil power for the purpose of taxation.[6]   Others obtained from the Arabs the privilege of farming the revenues derived from Christian taxation, and cruelly oppressed their coreligionists.[7]

These nefarious measures were backed up, even if they

---

[1] He was not defeated in his last battle, as is generally stated in histories.—See Al Makkari, ii. 197.

[2] Florez, "Esp. Sagr.," xviii. 312.   [3] *Ibid.*, xvii. 244.

[4] "Praesidali manu fultus." Samson, ii. Pref. sec. 2.   [5] *Ibid.*

[6] *Ibid.*, and Eulog., "Mem. Sanct.," iii. c. iv. sec. 5.   [7] Eul., l.l.

were not instigated, by Servandus, the Christian Count of
Cordova. He was the son of a serf of the Church,[1] and
married a cousin of Hostegesis.[2] Instead of champion-
ing the cause of the Christians, as his position should have
impelled him to do, he went so far in the opposite direction
as to call them up before him, and try to shake their attach-
ment to Christianity—a religion, nominally at least, his own
also. Those who held firm he forced to pay increased
taxes, and even levied blackmail on the churches. He did
not scruple to drag forth the bodies of martyrs from under
the altars of churches, and, showing them to the king, to
remind him that it had been forbidden to Christians to bury
their martyrs.[3]

Following up the hostile measures instituted by Hostegesis against Samson and Valentius, he proceeded to accuse
them of inciting the fanatics to revile Mohammed, urging
that they should be tested with this dilemma. They should
be asked whether what the revilers said were true or not.
"If they answer, 'true,' let them be punished as well as the
reviler; if 'false,' bid them slay the man themselves; refusing which, you will know that they have aided and abetted
him to abuse your Prophet. In that case, give me permission, and I will slay the three myself."[4]

We have had occasion to mention one or two cases of
Church, and national, Councils held in Spain under the
Arabs, and it will be worth while to enumerate all the instances which are recorded, that we may contrast them
with those held under the Goths. It was one of the most
characteristic features of the Old Church in Spain that

---

[1] Dozy, ii. 268.

[2] Samson, "Apol.," ii. Pref. sec. 5.   [3] Samson, l.l.

[4] *Ibid.*, sec. 9. This same Servandus, the meanest of timeservers,
seeing the Sultan's (Abdallah's) cause failing, deserted to the rebel Omar
and his Christian following, and was killed at Polei (?)—Ibn Hayyan.,
apud Dozy, ii. 270. His Arab name was Sherbil, and he was beheaded at
Cordova by the Arabs.—See De Gayangos' note on Al Mak., ii. 451, 2.

it was united so closely with the civil power as almost to render the Government of Spain a theocracy. This intimate connection of Church and State was naturally overthrown by the Arab conquest; but the Moslem rulers, seeing how useful such institutions as general councils were likely to be in adjusting the relations between Mussulmans and Christians, both allowed purely ecclesiastical councils to be called under their jurisdiction, and also summoned others in which they took part themselves, together with Jews, to the great scandal of the stricter Christians.[1]

To the purely ecclesiastical kind belong a council held at Seville by Elipandus [2] to condemn the errors of Migetius; and another, held by Cixila at Toledo in 776, against the errors of Egila, bishop of Elvira.[3] Whether Egila abjured his error is not known, but it is certain that he remained bishop.

Elipandus is also said, but on very doubtful authority, to have held a council, whereat he renounced his own error of Adoptionism.[4]

But the other class of councils, partly ecclesiastical and partly political, seem to have been commoner, and we have already seen how Reccafredus, Bishop of Seville, in conjunction with the Moslem authorities, held such a council, in order to coerce the fanatical party among the Christians; and we have a more particular account of another, which was held by Hostegesis, Bishop of Malaga, and Servandus,

---

[1] We even find in 962 that the bishops of Toledo and Cordova had Moslem names, viz., Obeidollah ibn Kasim (Al Makkari, ii. 162), and Akbar ibn Abdallah. Dozy, iii. 99.

[2] The exact date is unknown. Fleury, ii. p. 235.

[3] " Pseudo Luitprand," sec. 236, says—"Ad concilium ex omnibus Hispaniae partibus concurrunt." See also Pope Adrian I.'s Letter to the bishops of Spain in 785. Very little is known of this Egila, nor is it certain of what see he was the bishop.

[4] See below, p. 131 ad fin. and 166 ff.

Count of Cordova.[1] This council seems to have had some connection with the preceding one under Reccafredus, for Servandus was a strong and unscrupulous opponent of the party led by Eulogius, while Samson was their devoted supporter, though he did not carry his opinions so far as to suffer martyrdom in his own person. Samson was now accused of heresy [2] and sacrilege, as has been already mentioned. Hostegesis forced his views on the assembled bishops by the help of the secular arm, and a sentence of anathema and deposition was accordingly pronounced against the unfortunate Abbot.[3] One of the apparently consenting bishops was Valentius, Bishop of Cordova, but his judgement had evidently been coerced, for after the close of the council he sounded the other consenting bishops, and some who had not attended, as to their opinions, and found that most of them were ready to affirm Samson's orthodoxy, and a memorial was drawn up to that effect. This action of Valentius' brought upon him also a sentence of deposition, and he was succeeded by Stephanus Flaccus,[4]—the election of the latter being quite informal, as no metropolitan assisted thereat,[5] and neither the clergy nor laymen of his diocese made a petition in his favour.

This fresh deposition was formally sanctioned by a new council, held at the church of St Acislus; Flaccus, and some of those who had sided with Valentius, but were now terrified into submission, being in attendance; while the places of those who refused to come were taken by Jews and Mos-

---

[1] Samson, "Apol.," ii. Pref.

[2] On the ground, among others, that he recognised "nescio quam similitudines (besides the Trinity) non creaturas sed creatores." These appear (chap. ix.) to have been merely qualities, such as wisdom, etc. See Samson, chap. iii.

[3] "Indiscreta simplicitate et metu impiorum in superbiae fascibus sedentium."—*Ibid.* Samson was rendered incapable of holding office, or even of belonging to the Church.—*Ibid.*

[4] In 864.   [5] See above, p. 8.

lems.[1] These high-handed proceedings nearly led to an open rupture in the Church.[2]

In 914 a council is said to have been held (but on doubtful authority) by Orontius of Toledo,[3] and twenty years later by Basilius of Cordova. These would fall under the reign of the greatest of the Umeyyade Khalifs of Spain.[4]

——o——

CHAPTER VII.

SPAIN UNDER ABDURRAHMAN III.

ABDURRAHMAN III., Annasir Lidinillah (912-961), may be looked upon as the Solomon of the Spanish Sultans. Succeeding to the throne when quite a youth, to the exclusion of his uncles, the sons of the late Sultan, he found the country torn by innumerable factions, and the king's power openly defied by rebels, Arab, Berber, and Christian. In person, and through his generals, he put down all these rebels, and though not uniformly successful against the Christians in the North, yet he defeated them in a series of great engagements.[5] He welded all the discordant elements under his rule into one great whole,[6] thereby giving the Arab domination in Spain another lease of life. In 929 he took the title of Amir al Mumenin, or Commander of the Faithful. His alliance was sought by the Emperor of the East,[7] and he treated on equal terms

[1] Sayones (?) in the Latin. Samson, chap. iii.   [2] *Ibid.*, sec. 10.
[3] "Pseudo Luit.," sec. 328.   [4] *Ibid.* sec. 341.
[5] Mutonia (918); Calaborra; Vale de Junqueras (921).
[6] Dozy, ii. 351, from an Arab writer.
[7] A very interesting account of this embassy from Constantine VII. (947) is given in Al Makkari, ii. 137, from Ibn Khaldun.—See Conde, i. 442.

with the Emperor of Germany and the King of France.
To this great king, with more truth than to his namesake
Abdurrahman II., may be applied the words of Miss
Yonge :—[1]

"He was of that type of Eastern monarch, that seems
moulded on the character of Solomon—large-hearted, wise,
magnificent, tolerant, and peaceful. He was as great a
contrast to the stern, ascetic, narrow-minded, but earnest
Alfonso or Ramiro, as were the exquisite horse-shoe arches,
filagree stonework lattices, inlaid jewellery of marble pave-
ments, and slender minarets, to their dark vault-like, low-
browed churches, and solid castles built out of hard
unmanageable granite."

We find in this king none of that suspicious jealousy
which we saw in Mohammed, even though Omar, the arch
rebel, and Christian renegade, still held out at Bobastro,
when he ascended the throne; and his treatment of Christians was, throughout his reign, tolerant and politic.

But his claims in this respect will be best seen from a
very interesting fragment that has come down to our own
times, describing the embassy of a certain John of Gorz, a
monk from an abbey near Metz, who carried letters from
Otho, emperor of Germany, to the Spanish Sultan.[2]

In 950 Abdurrahman had sent an embassy to the emperor. A bishop who had been at the head of this embassy
died, and this seems to have caused a delay in the answer.
As the Khalif's letter contained blasphemies against Christ,
it was determined to write a reply in the king's name, such
as might perhaps convince Abdurrahman of the error of his
ways. A certain bishop, Adalbero, was appointed to be at
the head of the return embassy,[3] and he asks the abbot of
the monastery of Gorz to give him two assistants. Two

---

[1] P. 57.

[2] See "Vita Johannis Abbatis Gorziensis," 973, by John, Abbot of
Arnulph. "Migne," vol. cxxxvii., pp. 239-310.   [3] In 953.

are chosen, but one of these quarrels with his superior, and is expelled from the body; whereupon John offers himself as a substitute. The abbot only gives his consent to John's going with great reluctance, knowing that the young monk had an ardent longing to be a martyr, if he could only get the opportunity.

Going through Lyons, and by ship to Barcelona, the ambassadors reached the frontier town, Tortosa, and at last got to Cordova, where they were assigned a house two miles from the palace, and, though well entertained, were informed, to their dismay, that, as the Moorish ambassadors had been made to wait three years for an answer, Otho's messengers would have to wait nine years. Moreover, they now discovered that the king had been already apprised of the contents of the letter, which Otho had sent, by a comrade of the late ambassador-bishop, whom John and his companions had taken with them to Barcelona.

The king employs Hasdai, a Jew, as his go-between; who warns them not to divulge the contents of the letter, as it would make them liable to punishment; for the letter contained what Moslems would consider blasphemy against their Prophet. Soon after this John, the Bishop of Cordova, is sent to them to suggest that they should carry their gifts to the king, and say nothing of the letter. But John of Gorz stoutly refused to do this, saying that the delivery of the letter was his chief duty, and that as Abdurrahman had begun by reviling Christ, he must not be surprised at Otho's retaliating against Mohammed. However, John of Cordova begs him to remember the position in which the Christians stood, viz., under Pagan rule. "We are forbidden," he said, "by the apostle to resist the powers that be. In our calamity, we have this one consolation, we are allowed to observe our own laws and rites, and our rulers, if they see us diligent in our religion, honour us, cherish us, and delight in our society, while they abhor the Jews. As our religion, then, suffers no harm at their hands, let us obey the Moslems in other things." The bishop was anxious, there- fore, that the letter should be suppressed, as calculated to do harm to the Christian community, and no good to Otho. His advice, however, fell on deaf ears. The monk of Gorz was resolved on doing what he deemed his plain duty; nor was he content to forego his chance of martyrdom, though his action might entail disastrous consequences on the Christians subject to the Moors. He taunted the bishop with giving his advice from a fear of man. "Better die of hunger than eat the salt of unbelievers;" and expressed horror at the fact that the bishop was circumcised, and also abstained from certain meats in deference to Moslem scruples. It was in vain that the bishop pointed out that otherwise they could not live with the Saracens.

John of Gorz now expressed his intention of delivering the letter forthwith; but the king denied the ambassadors an audience, leaving them to themselves for six or seven weeks. Early in 955, however, the king sent to them, and asked if they held firm to their previous resolve, and on receiving an answer in the affirmative, he threatened all the Christians in his dominions with loss of privileges and even death. John of Gorz merely answers that the guilt would be on the king's head; but the latter is persuaded to milder counsels by his advisers, who remind him of Otho's power, and the certainty that he would interfere in favour of his ambassadors.

John of Gorz now proposes the only practicable course, that Abdurrahman should send a fresh embassy to Otho and ask for instructions for his ambassadors under the cir- cumstances. Recemundus,[1] a Christian, offers to go as

---

[1] De Gayangos, on Al Makkari, ii. p. 464, identifies him with Rabi, a bishop mentioned as an ambassador of Abdurrahman III. in Al Makkari, i. 236, ii. 139; but Rabi may have been the bishop

ambassador, if a vacant bishopric be given him as a reward.
He sets out and reaches Gorz in February 956. Otho gives
him a fresh letter, with instructions to suppress the former
one, to conclude an alliance with the Sultan, and make an
arrangement with him for putting down the brigands who
infested the marches.

Leaving Gorz with Dudo, the emperor's legate, on March
30, he reached Cordova on June 1st, but the Sultan declined
to receive the second comers till he had received the earlier
embassy. So, after three years semi-captivity, John is released, and told to prepare himself for the king's presence
by shaving, washing, and putting on new apparel. He de-
clines to go in any otherwise than he is; and even when the
king, thinking his refusal due to poverty, sends him a sum
of money, the monk accepts the gift and distributes it to the
poor, but says he will only see the king as a poor monk.
The king good-naturedly said: "Let him come as he likes."
On June 21, 956, the ambassadors were conducted to the
king's presence along a road thronged with sight-seers. The
steps of the palace were laid down with tapestry, and a
guard of honour lined both sides of the approach. On
John's entrance, the king, as a great mark of distinction,
gave him his open palm to kiss, and beckoned him to a
seat near his own couch. After a silence Abdurrahman
apologised to the monk for the long delay which he had
been obliged to impose on the embassy, and which was in
no sense due to disrespect for John himself, whose virtue
and wisdom he could not but acknowledge. As a proof
that this was no mere empty compliment, the king expressed
his readiness to give him whatever he asked. John's wrath
vanishes at these gracious words, and they talk amicably
together. But when the monk asks leave to depart Abdurrahman says:—"After waiting so long to see one another,

who died during the embassy to Otho. Recemundus, as De Gayangos
(l.l.) says, was a katib or clerk of the palace.

shall we part so soon?" He suggests that they should
have at least three interviews. At their next meeting they
discourse on the respective power of the empires of Otho
and the Khalif himself; and the Sultan, taught by the ex-
perience of Spain, points out the unwisdom of allowing
feudal subjects to become too powerful, by dividing kingdoms between them.

So ends this unique and interesting fragment, which
throws so pleasant a light on the character and the Court
of the greatest of Spanish Sultans, and proves that the
Christians at that time enjoyed considerable freedom, and
even honour, at the hands of the Moslem Government.

The reason why the king was unwilling to receive the
first letter brought by John was not so much because he
was reluctant to read words against Mohammed, as because
he would by so doing render himself liable to the penalty of
death, which was ordained by law to any Moslem—king or
slave—who listened to abuse of the Prophet without exact-
ing summary vengeance from the blasphemer. But—and here
was the king's dilemma—he could not punish the ambassadors without incurring the enmity of Otho. The only
possible alternative was that suggested by John, that Otho
should be asked to withdraw the objectionable letter, without the Sultan having officially read it, and this Abdurrahman adopted. The moderation of the king is conspicuous
throughout, for we must regard the threat against the
Christians as merely a threat, never really intended to be
put into execution.

In showing tolerance towards their Christian subjects, the
Spanish khalifs might be thought to have forgotten the
traditions of Islam; but, as a matter of fact, Mohammed
seems to have been very inconsistent in his views with
regard to Christians and Jews at different times of his
career, and while he enjoined the necessity of Holy Wars,[1]

[1] Tradition attributes even stronger approval of Holy Wars to

he permitted the people of the book to be admitted to tribute.[1]   In one passage he even seems to allow the possibility of salvation to Jews, Christians, and Sabians : " Verily they who believe, and those who Judaize, and the Sabians, and the Christians—whoever of these believeth in God and the last day, and doeth that which is right—there shall come no fear on them, neither shall they be grieved." [2]   And there is one remarkable text to find in the mouth of Mohammed, " Let there be no violence in religion." [3]

Moreover, some of the best Mohammedan rulers that have ever lived upheld the same principle of toleration. Abbas II., one of the Persian Sufis, is reported to have said : " It is for God, not for me, to judge of men's consciences, and I will never interfere with what belongs to the tribunal of the great Creator and Lord of the Universe." [4] Again, Akbar, one of the greatest kings that ever lived, followed in practice the principle thus expressed by his minister, Abul Fazl : " Persecution after all defeats its own ends ; it obliges men to conceal their opinions, but produces no change in them." [5]   Noble sentiments surely, and such as we should expect from followers of Christ rather than of Mohammed !

Yet far too often have portions of the Christian Church been conspicuous for intolerance rather than tolerance.   Alcuin, indeed, does say in his letter to Aquila, Bishop of Winchester, that he does not approve of punishing heresy with death, because God, by the mouth of His

---

Mohammed than can be found in the Koran,—*e.g.*, " The sword is the key of Paradise and Hell.   A drop of blood shed in the cause of God, a night spent in arms, are of more avail than two months of fasting and prayer.   Whoever falls in battle against the infidel, his sins are forgiven him."   [1] Koran, xlvii., ad init.

[2] Koran, v., v. 73.   This may be said in the general sense of Acts x. 35.   [3] Koran, ii., v. 258.

[4] See Freeman's " Saracens," p. 230 ; from Malcolm's " Persia," i. p 583.   [5] *Ibid.*, from " Ayeen Akbery," p. 11.

prophet, had said : " I have no pleasure in the death of the wicked, but that the wicked turn from his way and live ; "[1] but Alcuin was a man of unusual mildness and sweet reasonableness, as his letters to Felix and Elipandus testify. On the other hand, there were too many frantic bigots in the Church, like Arnold of Citeaux, whose impious words, in connection with the massacre of Albigensians, are not likely to be forgotten—" Slay all ; God will know His own."

In fact, so opposed did the Christian spirit come to be to the Mohammedan in this respect, that their toleration was made a principal argument against the Moors by the Archbishop of Valencia in his memorial to Philip III. at the end of the sixteenth century.[2]

A very melancholy instance of bigotry and intolerance is afforded by Bernard, a French monk, who was made Archbishop of Toledo by Alfonso, on the capture of that city in 1085. By the treaty of capitulation certain mosques had been expressly reserved to the Moslems, just in the same way as certain churches had been reserved for the Christians by Musa in 712. But Bernard, by way of showing his zeal in the cause of God, in defiance of the king's plighted word, chose to perform mass in the chief mosque. Alfonso was furiously angry when he heard of his archbishop's proceedings, but the Moslems, with wonderful forbearance, seeing that the king had not authorised Bernard's outrageous conduct, came forward of their own accord and begged him to pardon the act, and even voluntarily surrendered their mosque.[3]

Not only were the Christians allowed to practise their religion, but even, as we have seen above, encouraged in it.[4] Almanzor, the champion of Islam, allowed his Christian

---

[1] Ezekiel xxxiii. 11.   [2] Prescott, "Ferd. and Isab.," p. 376, n.
[3] Mariana, ix. 10.
[4] See p. 57. Recent history affords a similar instance from the Christian side. See "Gordon in Central Africa," p. 54—"I have

servants to rest on Sundays. Christians in every reign held high posts at court[1] and throughout the land, and not only timeserving Christians but men like Samson and Leovigild, who were known to sympathise with the party of zealots, were employed by the king to write letters to, and negotiate with, the neighbouring kings. This was no doubt due to their general trustworthiness, their quickness, and their knowledge of Arabic as well as Latin.

Among the great functionaries of state there was one who held the office of Kitabatu-dh-dhimam, which, being interpreted, is "the office of protection." The Christians and Jews were under his general jurisdiction, and were called "the people of the protection."[2] But besides this Arab "Secretary of State for the Christians," the latter had their own counts—a relic of the Gothic system—who, however, did not always stand up for their interests.[3] There were also Christian censors,[4] but it is not known what position they held in the State.

The young Christian cadets of noble birth were brought up at Court, and numbers of Sclavonian Christians served in the king's bodyguard, of whom under Hakem I. (796-822) there were 2000.[5]

All things considered, it is a matter for surprise that these two peoples, so unlike in race, habits, prejudices, and religion, lived so comparatively quietly side by side in spite of a perpetual state of warfare between the Arabs and the

made them make a mosque, and keep the Ramadhan." *Ibid.*, p. 249, "I had the mosque cleared out and restored for worship, and endowed the priests and crier, and had a great ceremony at the opening of it. . . . They blessed me and cursed Zebehr Pasha who took the mosque from them. To me it appears that the Mussulman worships God as well as I do, and is as acceptable, if sincere, as any Christian."

[1] Such as secretary, farmer of taxes, or even prime minister.

[2] Al Makk., i. p. 103 ; and De Gayangos' note, p. 398.

[3] *E.g.*, Servandus. Cp. also Cyprianus.   [4] See above, p. 49.

[5] Conde, i. p. 260.

Christians in the North, which tended to keep alive the animosities of the two races in that part of Spain which was under Mohammedan rule.[1] Moreover, the pride of race was very strong in the pure-blooded Arabs. Thus the poet Said ibn Djoud, in a poem called the " battle of the town " (Polei), boasts that the conquerors are of the pure race of Adnan and Kahtan, without any foreign admixture ; while he calls the defeated Spaniards miscreants, followers of a false faith,[2] sons of the pale-faces. The haughty Arabs, in fact, were too prone to look upon all the Spaniards, both renegades and Christians, as mere canaille.[3]

But, in spite of this, the races to a certain extent amalgamated ; and Eulogius endeavours to prove that, but for the outbreak of fanaticism in the middle of the ninth century, this amalgamation would have had serious results for Christianity in Spain.[4]

The Arabs did not disdain to seek the alliance of the free Christian States, nor were the latter averse from doing the same, when political occasion demanded it. As early as 798 the Walis of the frontier cities sought to make themselves independent by what the Arab writer describes as " vile policy and unworthy acts," *i.e.*, by seeking the friendship of the Christian kings ;[5] and there are many instances of these kings asking aid, even servilely, from Arab princes.[6]

---

[1] Dozy, ii. 108, puts the distinction between the races very forcibly :—"Ce peuple qui joignait à une gaîté franche et vive une sensualité raffinée devait inspirer aux prêtres, qui aimaient les retraites éternelles et profondes, les grands renoncéments et les terribles expiations, une répugnance extrême et invincible."

[2] Dozy, ii. 223.

[3] " C'était leur terme consacrée." Dozy, ii. 211.

[4] " Heu pro dolor ! quia esse sub Gentibus delicias computamus, iugumque cum infidelibus ducere non renitimur. Et inde ex cotidiano usu illorum sacrilegiis plerumque utimur et magis ipsorum contubernia affectamus."—Eul., " Doc. Martyr," sec. 18.

[5] Conde, i. 244 : " Chron. Alb.," vi. sec. 58 : " Chron. Lib.," sec. 30.

[6] Al Makkari, ii. 161, Ordono the Bad and Hakem II.

Again, as was inevitable from the nature of the case, inter-marriages were common between the two races. The example was early set by the widow of Roderic, the last Gothic king, marrying Abdulazìz, son of Musa. The sons of Witiza also married Arab women, and Sarah, the daughter of one of these princes, was the progenetrix of a noble family of Arabs, one of her descendants being the historian, Ibn al Kuttiya, which means son of the Gothic princess.[1] Abdur-rahman Anassir, the greatest of all the Spanish Sultans, was the son of a Christian slave, named Maria,[2] and the mighty Almanzor had for grandmother the daughter of a renegade Christian.[3] These are some instances, but it is not neces-sary to dwell on what was so common an occurrence as intermarriage between the peoples, and is forbidden neither by the Koran,[4] nor by the Bible.

However, there is one point in this connection which deserves a more particular notice. The intermingling of the races has been supposed to have been facilitated in part by the yearly tribute of 100 maidens paid by the northern kings to the earlier Arab Sultans. Modern historians mostly throw doubt upon the story, saying that of the early historians none mention it, and that the Arabs do not even allude to it.[5] But if Conde is to be trusted, an Arab writer does speak of it, as of a thing well known. In a letter of Omar[6] ibn Alaftaṣ Almudafar, King of Algarve, to Alfonso VI., in 1086, occur the words :—" Do thou remember the time of Mohammed Almanzor, and bring to thy mind those treaties wherein thy forefathers offered him the homage even

---

[1] Al Makkari, ii. 15, 22, and De Gayangos' note, p. 454.

[2] Conde, i. 364.   [3] Dozy, iii. 124.

[4] Koran, v. 5 :—" Ye are allowed to marry free women of those that have received the Scriptures before you."

[5] Dunham, ii. 131: Romey's "Histoire d'Espagne," iii. 276.

[6] Conde, ii. 238: Al Makkari, ii. 256, calls him Omar ibn Mohammed etc ibn Alafthas Almutawakkel, King of Badajos.

of their own daughters, and sent him those damsels in tribute even to the land of our rule."

The maiden tribute is the subject of several ancient ballads by the Christian Spaniards. The following are two verses from one of these :—

> " For he who gives the Moorish king a hundred maids of Spain
> Each year when in the season the day comes round again ;
> If he be not a heathen he swells the heathen's train—
> 'Twere better burn a kingdom than suffer such disdain !

> " If the Moslems must have tribute, make men your tribute-money,
> Send idle drones to tease them within their hives of honey ;
> For, when 'tis paid with maidens, from every maid there spring
> Some five or six strong soldiers to serve the Moorish king."[1]

Southey also says that the only old Portuguese ballad known to him was on this subject. The evidence, then, of the ballads is strong for a fact of this kind, telling, too, as it does, so much against the writers of the ballads.[2]

As to the Christian chroniclers, it is quite true that we find no mention of this tribute in the history of Sebastian of Salamanca and the Chronicle of Albeldum, but there is a direct allusion to it in a document included in the collection of Florez.[3] "Our ancestors," says Ramiro, "the kings of the land—we blush to record it—to free themselves from the raids of the Saracens, consented to pay them yearly a shameful tribute of a hundred maidens distinguished for their beauty, fifty of noble birth, and fifty from the people." It was to put an end to this nefarious tribute that Ramiro now ordered a levy *en masse*. This, if the document is genuine (and Florez gives no hint to the contrary), is good evidence

---

[1] Lockhart.

[2] Unless the ballads were written later than 1250—*i.e.*, after Rodrigo of Toledo had made the story known by his history.

[3] " España Sagrada," xix. 329 — " Privilegium quod dicitur votorum, anno 844 a rege Ranemiro I., ecclesiae B. Jacobi concessae."

G

for the fact. Many succeeding writers mention it. Lucas of Tuy[1] says that Ramiro was asked for the tribute in 842. Johannes Vasaeus[2] speaks of it, as also Alfonso, Bishop of Burgos ;[3] and lastly, Rodrigo of Toledo[4] says that Mauregatus (783-788), having obtained the throne of Leon by Saracen help, agreed to send this tribute yearly.

On the whole, then, the evidence is in favour of the maiden tribute being no myth, but of its having been regularly paid for more than fifty years. Most of these Christian maidens probably embraced the religion of their husbands, but in some cases they no doubt converted them to their own faith.

From different causes, some of which will be mentioned elsewhere, conversions were frequent from one religion to the other. Motives of worldly interest naturally caused the balance in these to fall very much against the Christians, but as the Mohammedan power declined the opposite was the case. Though voluntary apostasy was, and is, unpardonable, Mohammed seems to have made allowances for those who apostatized under compulsion ; for when one of his followers, Ammar ibn Yaser, being tortured by the Koreish, renounced his belief in God and in Mohammed's mission, but afterwards came weeping to the Prophet, Mohammed received him kindly, and, wiping his eyes, said : "What fault was it of thine, if they forced thee?"[5]

---

[1] Lucas Tudensis, "Chronicon Mundi," bk. iv.
[2] "Hispaniae Chronicon," 783 A.D.
[3] "Anacephalaiosis," sec. 51.   [4] III. c. 7.
[5] Koran, xvi. ver. 109, Sale's note.

———o———

CHAPTER VIII.

THE MUWALLADS.

THAT the conversions from Christianity to Islam were very numerous at first we can sufficiently gather from the fact that the new converts formed a large and important party in the State, and almost succeeded in wresting the government of Spain from the Arabs. The disorder and civil war which may almost be said to have been chronic in Spain during the Arab dominion were due to the fact that three distinct races settled in that country were striving for the mastery, each of these races being itself divided into two bitterly hostile factions. The Arabs were split up into the two factions of Yemenite or Beladi Arabs, the descendants of Kahtan, and Modharites, the Arabs of Mecca and Medina, who claimed descent from Adnan.[1] To the latter section belonged the reigning family of Umeyyades. The Berbers, who looked upon themselves as the real conquerors of Spain, and whose numbers were subsequently reinforced by fresh immigrations, were composed of two hostile tribes of Botar and Beranis. Thirdly, there were the Spaniards, part Christian, part Mohammedan; the latter being either renegades themselves or the descendants of renegades These apostates were called by the Arabs Mosalimah, or New Moslems,[2] and their descendants Muwallads,[3] or those not of Arabic origin. The Christians were either tribute-paying Christians, called Ahlu dh dhimmah; or free Christians, under Moslem supremacy, called Ajemi;[4] or apostates

---

[1] See above, p. 23, note 3.
[2] Cp. " New Christians."
[3] Pronounced Mulads, hence Mulatto. The word means "adopted."
[4] Al Makkari, ii. 446. De Gayangos' note.

from Islam,[1] called Muraddin.   The Muwallads, in spite of
the Mohammedan doctrine of the equality and brotherhood
of Moslems, were looked down upon with the utmost contempt by the pure-blooded Arabs.[2]   Their condition was
even worse than that of the Christians, for they were, generally speaking, excluded from lucrative posts, and from all
administration of affairs—a dangerous policy, considering
that they formed a majority of the population.[3]   Stronger
and more humane than the Berbers, they were friends of
order and civilization.   Intellectually they were even
superior to the conquering Arabs.[4]

The natural result of their being Spaniards by race, and
Arabs by religion, was that they sided now with one faction
and now with another, and at one time, under the weak
Abdallah (888-912), were the mainstay of the Sultan against
his rebellious subjects.   After breaking with the Sultan they
almost succeeded in gaining possession of the whole kingdom, and carried fire and desolation to the very gates of
Cordova.[5]

As early as 805 the Muwallads of Cordova, incited by
certain theologians, revolted under Hakem I., but the rising
was suppressed.   In 814, however, they again rose, and the
rebellion being put down with great severity by the help
of the Berbers, the Cordovan Muwallads were exiled, 1500
going to Alexandria, and 8000 to Fez.[6]   But though exter-

---

[1] Al Makkari, ii. 458.

[2] Cp. "Gordon in Central Africa," p. 300.   ". . . the only regret
is that I am a Christian.   Yet they would be the first to despise me if
I recanted and became a Mussulman." An Arab poet calls them "sons
of slaves," Dozy, ii. 258.

[3] So Dozy, ii. p. 52.   But perhaps he meant "of the Arab population."

[4] Dozy, ii. 261.

[5] Al Makkari, ii. p. 458.   De Gayangos' note.

[6] Dozy, App. B to vol. ii.   Hakem was called Al rabadhi (= he of
the suburb) from this.

minated in Cordova, the renegades still mustered strong in Spain. At Elvira they rose in Abdallah's reign, under a chief named Nabil, and threw off the Arab yoke;[1] and, previously to this, Abdurrahman ibn Merwan ibn Yunas and Sadoun had headed similar revolts at Badajos and Merida.[2] At Seville the Muwallad element was specially strong, as we see from the many family names, such as Beni Angelino, Beni Sabarico, which betray a Spanish origin. The majority of the inhabitants embraced Islam early, and had their mosque by the middle of the ninth century, but they retained many Spanish customs and characteristics. When the Arabs of Seville revolted against the Sultan, the renegade party joined the latter. At Saragoza, the Beni Kasi, descendants of a noble Gothic family, set up an independent kindgom, waging war indifferently with all their neighbours.

It does not come within the scope of this inquiry to trace out the history of all the revolts made by the Arabs or Berbers against the Sultan's authority, but the policy and position of the Muwallads and Christians are a necessary part of our subject. The latter, though well treated on the whole, naturally looked back with regret to the days of their own supremacy, and were ready to intrigue with anyone able to assist them against their Arab rulers. Accordingly we find them communicating with the kings of France; and there is still extant a letter from Louis the Débonnaire to the people of Merida, written in 826, which is as follows :—
"We have heard of your tribulation, which you suffer from the cruelty of your king Abdurrahman, who has tried to take away your goods, and has oppressed you just as his father Abulaz did. He, making you pay unjust taxes, which you were not bound to pay, turned you from friends into

---

[1] Ibn Hayyan, apud Al Makkari, ii. 446, ff.
[2] In 875. "Chron Albel.," sec. 62. Dozy, ii. 184.

enemies, and from obedient to disobedient vassals, inasmuch as he infringed your liberties. But you, like brave men, we hear, are resisting the tyrant, and we write now to condole with you, and to exhort you to continue your resistance, and since your king is our enemy as well as yours, let us join in opposing him.

"We purpose to send an army to the frontier next summer to wait there till you give us the signal for action. Know then that, if you will desert him and join us, your ancient liberties shall be secured to you, and you shall be free of all taxes and tributes, and shall live under your own laws."[1]

The army promised was sent under the king's son, but seems to have effected nothing.

During the period of religious disturbance at Cordova, when the voluntary martyrdoms became so frequent, and just at the time of Mohammed's accession, the Christians of Toledo, encouraged, we may suppose, by their proximity to the free Christians, revolted in favour of their coreligionists at Cordova. No wonder then that Mohammed imagined that the outbreak of fanaticism in Cordova was but the signal for a general mutiny of his Christian subjects. As we have already seen, the king set out with an army against the Toledans, who appealed to Ordono I. of Leon for help. Glad enough to get such an opportunity for weakening the Arab government, Ordono sent a large auxiliary force, but the Toledans and Leonnese were defeated with great slaughter by the Sultan's troops.[2] Within twenty years, however, Toledo became practically independent, except for the payment of tribute.[3]

From all this it will be clear that the Spanish part of the population, whether Moslem or Christian, was opposed to the exclusiveness of the old Arabs, and ready to make

---

[1] Apud Florez, " Españo Sagrada." [2] Dozy, ii. 162.
[3] *Ibid*, p. 182.

common cause against them. The unity of race prevailed over the difference of creed, as it did in the case of the English Roman Catholics in the war with Spain, and as it usually will under such circumstances. The national party were fortunate enough to find an able leader in the person of the celebrated rebel, Omar ibn Hafsun, who came near to wresting the sovereignty of Spain from the hands of the Umeyyades. Omar was descended from a Count Alfonso,[1] and his family had been Christians till the apostasy of his grandfather Djaffar. Omar, being a wild unmanageable youth, took up the lucrative and honourable profession of bandit, his headquarters being at Bobastro or Bishter, a stronghold somewhere between Archidona and Ronda, in the sierra stretching from Granada to Gibraltar.[2] After a brief sojourn in Africa, where his ambition was inflamed by a prophecy announcing a great future, he returned to Spain, and at once began business again as brigand at Bobastro with nearly 6000 men.[3] Being captured, he was brought to Cordova, but spared on condition of enlisting in the king's forces. But he soon escaped from Cordova, and became chief of all the Spaniards in the South, Moslem and Christian,[4] whose ardour he aroused by such words as these : "Too long have you borne the yoke of the Sultan, who spoils you of your goods, and taxes you beyond your means. Will you let yourselves be trampled on by the Arabs, who look upon you as their slaves ? It is not ambition that prompts me to rebel, but a desire to avenge you and myself." To strengthen his cause he made alliances at

---

[1] Dozy, ii. 190.   [2] Al Makkari, ii. 437.   De Gayangos' note.
[3] In 880 or 881.
[4] See a description of him quoted by Stanley Lane-Poole ("Moors in Spain," p. 107) from an Arab writer : "Woe unto thee, Cordova ! when the captain with the great nose and ugly face—he who is guarded before by Moslems, and behind by idolaters—when Ibn Hafsun comes before thy gates. Then will thine awful fate be accomplished."

different times with the Muwallads in Elvira, Seville, and Saragoza, and with the successful rebel, Abdurrahman ibn Merwan, in Badajos.

Openly defying the Sultan's forces, he was only kept in check by Almundhir, the king's son, who succeeded his father in 886. Omar was further strengthened by the accession to his side of Sherbil, the Count of Cordova.[1] The death of Almundhir in 888 removed from Omar's path his only able enemy, and, during Abdallah's weak reign, the rebel leader was virtual king of the south and east of Spain. The district of Regio[2] was made over to him by the king, and Omar's lieutenant, Ibn Mastarna, was made chief of Priejo.

This protracted war, which was really one for national independence, was carried on year after year with varying success. At one time Omar conceived the intention of proclaiming the Abasside Khalifs,[3] at another he grasped at the royal power himself; and Abdallah's empire was only saved by a seasonable victory in 891 at Hisn Belay (or Espiel).[4] The battle was fought on the eve of the Passover, and the Moslems taunted their enemies with having such a joyful feast, and so many victims to commemorate it with. This shows that a large, perhaps the largest, part of Omar's army was Christian. Another indication of this is found in a poem of Tarikh ibn Habib,[5] where, speaking of the coming destruction of Cordova, he says: " The safest place will then be the hill of Abu Abdu, where once stood a church," meaning that Omar's Christian soldiers would respect that sanctuary, and no other. Indeed, it is certain

---

[1] Servandus. Al Makkari, ii. 456. De Gayangos' note.

[2] Where Islam was almost extinct. Dozy, ii. 335.

[3] Al Makkari, ii. p. 456. De Gayangos' note.

[4] Ibn Hayyan, apud Al Makk., ii. p. 452. This seems to be the same victory as that which Dozy (ii. 284) calls Polei or Aguilar.

[5] See Dozy, ii. p. 275.

that Omar himself became a Christian some time before this battle,[1] as his father had done before him. He took the name of Samuel, and his daughter Argentea, as we have seen, suffered martyrdom. This change of creed on Omar's part changed the character of the war, and gave it more of a religious,[2] and perhaps less of a national, character, for the Spanish Moslems fell off from him, when he became Christian and built churches.

Towards the close of his reign Abdallah was able to assert his supremacy, though Omar and his followers still held out. Omar himself did not die till 917, some years after Abdallah's death. The king's successor, Abdurrahman III., was a different stamp of man from Abdallah, and the reduction of Omar became only a question of time, though, in fact, the apostasy of Omar from Islam had made the ultimate success of the national party very doubtful, if not impossible. After Omar's death, his son, Djaffar, thought to recover the support of the Spanish Moslems by embracing Islam ; but he thereby lost the confidence of the Christians, by whom he was murdered. In 928 his brother Hafs surrendered, with Bobastro, to the Sultan, and the great rebellion was finally extinguished.

So ended the grand struggle of the national party, first under the direction of the Muwallads, and then of the Christians, to shake off the Arab and Berber yoke. During the remainder of the tenth century the strong administration of Abdurrahman III., Hakem II., and the great Almanzor, gave the Christians no chance of raising the cry of " Spain for the Spanish." The danger of a renewal of the rebellion once removed, the position of the Christians does not seem to have been made any worse in consequence of their late

[1] Ibn Hayyan, apud Dozy, ii. p. 326.
[2] In 896, on the capture of Cazlona by a renegade named Ibn as Khalia, all the Christians were massacred.—Dozy, ii. p. 327.

disaffection, and Abdurrahman, himself the son of a Christian mother, treated all parties in the revolt with great leniency, even against the wishes and advice of the more devout Moslems. Almanzor, too, made himself respected, and even liked, by his Christian subjects, and there is no doubt that his victories over the Christian States in the North[1] were won very largely with the aid of Christian soldiers. His death was the signal for the disruption of the Spanish Khalifate, and from 1010-1031, when the khalifate was finally extinguished, complete anarchy prevailed in Saracen Spain. The Berbers made a determined effort to regain their ascendency, and their forces, seconded by the Christians, succeeded in placing Suleiman on the throne in 1013. A succession of feeble rulers, set up by the different factions —Arab, Berber, and Slave—followed, until Hischem III. was forced to abdicate in 1031, and the Umeyyade dynasty came to an end, after lasting 275 years. By this time the Christians in the North had gathered themselves together for a combined advance against the Saracen provinces, never again to retrograde, scarcely even to be checked, till in 1492 fell Granada, the last stronghold of the Moors in Spain.[2]

[1] Al Makkari, ii. p. 214.

[2] In 1630 there was not a single Moslem left in Spain.—Al Makk., i. p. 74.

—o—

CHAPTER IX.

CHRISTIANS AND MOSLEMS IGNORANT OF ONE
ANOTHER'S CREED.

IN spite of the close contact into which the Christians and Mohammedans were brought in Spain, and the numerous conversions and frequent intermarriages between the two sections, no thorough knowledge seems to have existed, on either side, of the creed of the other party. Such, at least, is the conclusion to which we are driven, on reading the only direct records which remain on the subject among Arab and Christian writers. These on the Christian side consist chiefly of quotations from a book on Mohammedanism by the abbot Speraindeo in a work of his disciple, Eulogius;[1] and some rather incoherent denunciations of Mohammed and his religion by Alvar,[2] another pupil of the abbot's. In these, as might be expected, great stress is laid on the sensuality of Mohammed's paradise,[3] and the lewdness of the Prophet himself. As to the latter, though many of Gibbon's coarse sarcasms do not rest on good authority, very little can be said for the Prophet. But among other blasphemies attributed by Speraindeo to Mohammed is one of which we find no mention in the Koran—the assertion, namely, that he would in the next world be wedded to the Virgin Mary. John, Bishop of

---

[1] Eul., "Mem. Sanct.," i. sec. 7.

[2] Alvar, "Ind. Lum.," secs. 21-35.

[3] *Ibid.*, secs. 23, 24. Mohammed's paradise was by no means wholly sensual.—Sale's Koran. Introd., p. 78.

Seville, is equally incorrect when, in a letter to Alvar,[1] he alleges a promise on the part of Mohammed that he would, like Christ, rise again from the dead; whereas his body, being neglected by his relations, was devoured by dogs. The Christian bishop does not hesitate to add—sepultus est in infernum—he was buried in hell.[2]

It is generally supposed that Mohammed could neither read nor write, and this appears to have been the opinion of Alvar;[3] but the same witness acknowledges that the Koran was composed in such eloquent and beautiful language that even Christians could not help reading and admiring it.[4]

On the important question of Mohammed's position with regard to Christianity, Eulogius[5] at least formed a correct judgment. Mohammed, he tells us "blasphemously taught that Christ was the Word of God,[6] and His Spirit;[7] a great prophet,[8] endowed with much power from God;[9] like Adam in His creation,[10] but not equal to God (the Creator);[11] and that by reason of His blameless[12] life, being filled with the Holy Spirit,[13] He showed marvellous signs and wonders through the power of God,[14] not working by His own Godhead, but as a righteous Man, and an

---

[1] Sec. 9.

[2] This shows the hatred of Christians for Mohammed, whom, says Eulogius ("Mem. Sanct.," i. sec. 20), it would be every Christian's duty to kill, were he alive on earth.

[3] Alvar, "Ind. Lum," sec. 26.

[4] *Ibid.*, sec. 29. This is more than can be said at the present day.

[5] Eul., "Lib. Apol.," sec. 19.

[6] Koran, ch. iii. 40.

[7] Koran, ch. ii. 81, "strengthened with Holy Spirit."

[8] Kor., c. iii. 59.

[9] Kor., c. iii. 45.   [10] Kor., c. iii. 50.

[11] Kor., c. ix. 33.   [12] Kor., c. iii.

[13] This is a mistake of Eulogius. See Sale's note on Koran, ch. ii. 81, note.

[14] Kor., ch. v. 110 ff.

obedient servant,[1] obtaining much power and might from the Almighty God through prayer."

Alvar is much more unfair to Mohammed than his friend Eulogius, and he even seems to have had a prejudiced idea [2] that the Prophet set himself deliberately to preach doctrines the opposite of those taught by Christ. It would be nearer to the truth to say that the divergence between the two codes of morals was due to the natural ignorance of an illiterate Arabian, brought into contact only with an heretical form of Christianity, the real doctrines of which he was therefore not likely to know.

According to Alvar, the sixth day of the week was chosen for the Mohammedan holy day, because Christ suffered on that day. We shall realise the absurdity of this when we consider the reverence in which Mohammed held the very name of Christ, going so far even as to deny that Christ Himself was crucified at all.[8] The true reason for selecting Friday, as alleged by Mohammed himself, was, because the work of creation ended on that day.[4]

Again, sensuality was preached, says Alvar, because Christ preached chastity. But Mohammed cannot fairly be said to have preached sensuality, though his private life in this respect was by no means pure.

Gluttony was advocated instead of fasting. A more baseless charge was never made; for how can it be contended that Christianity enjoins fasting, while Islam disapproves of it, in the face of such texts as Matthew ix. 14,[5] and Isaiah lviii. 6—"Is not this the fast that I have chosen? To loose the bands of wickedness, to undo the heavy burdens, and to let the oppressed go free?" on the one hand; and on

---

[1] Koran, cc. iv. ad fin ; xliii. 59.   [2] See Dozy, ii. 107.

[3] See Koran, cc. iii. 47 ; iv. 157 ; and Sale's notes.

[4] See Sale's note on Koran, c. lxii. 9.

[5] Cf. also Matt. xi. 19—"The Son of Man came eating and drinking, and they say, Behold a gluttonous man and a wine-bibber."

the other the express injunction of the Koran[1] :—" O true
believers, a fast is ordained you, as it was ordained to those
before you . . . if ye fast, it will be better for you, if ye
knew it.   The month of Ramadan shall ye fast."   But Alvar
goes on to make a more astonishing statement still :—" Christ
ordained that men should abstain from their wives during
a fast, while Mohammed consecrated those days to carnal
pleasure."   Christ surely gives us no such injunction,
though St Paul does say something of the kind.   The
Koran[2] explicitly says—" It is lawful for you on the night
of the fast to go in unto your wives; they are a garment
unto you, and you are a garment unto them."   We even
find an incident recorded by an Arabian writer, where
Yahya ibn Yahya, the famous faqui, imposed a penance
of a month's extra fast on Abdurrahman II. (822-852) for
violating the Prophet's ordinance, that wives should be
abstained from during the fasting month.[3]   Alvar, being a
layman, may perhaps be supposed not to have studied Mohammedanism critically, and that his zeal was not according
to knowledge is perhaps the best explanation of the matter.
In one place[4] he informs us of his intention of writing a
book on the Cobar,[5] but the work, if ever written, has not
survived.   Nor is this much to be regretted, if we may judge
by the wild remarks he indulges in elsewhere[6] on this theme.
In that passage he seems to apply the obscure prophecy of
Daniel[7] to Mohammed, forgetting that verse 37 speaks of
one who "shall regard not the desire of women," a description hardly characteristic of Mohammed.   He identifies the
God Maozim (Hebr. Mauzim), which our revised version
(v. 38) translates the "God of fortresses" with the Mo-

---

[1] Chapter ii. 180.
[2] Chapter ii. 185.   The Mohammedan fast is confined to the day time.
[3] From Ibn Khallekan, apud Dozy, ii. 108.
[4] " Ind. Lum.," sec. 25.   [5] *I.e.*, the Caaba apparently.
[6] " Ind. Lum.," sec. 25, ff.   [7] C. xi. vv. 21, ff.

hammedan Cobar;[1] and the strange god, whom he shall acknowledge, Alvar identifies with the devil which inspired the Prophet in the guise of the angel Gabriel. All this, as the writer himself allows, is very enigmatical.

Alvar does not scruple even to accuse the Moslems of idolatry, asserting that the Arabian tribes worship their idol (the Caaba black stone[2]) as they used to do of yore, and that they set apart a holy month, Al Mozem, in honour of this idol.[3]

Finally, Mohammed is spoken of variously as the precursor of Antichrist,[4] or as Antichrist himself.[5]

Let us now see how far we can gather the opinions of educated Moslems with regard to Christian doctrine and worship. If we find these to be no less one-sided and erroneous than the opinions of Christians as to Mohammedanism, yet can we the more easily excuse the Moslems, for the Koran itself, the very foundation and guide of all their religious dogmas, is full of incorrect and inconsistent notions on the subject.

The most important of these mistakes was that the Christians worshipped a Trinity of Deities—God, Christ, Mary.[6] The inclusion of the Virgin Mary into this Trinity was perhaps due to the fact that worship was paid to her even at that early date, as it certainly is among the Roman Catholics at this day. As will have been seen from a passage quoted above,[7] something very like adoration was already paid to the Virgin in the churches of Spain.

---

[1] ? Caaba.   [2] Sale, Introduction to Koran, p. 91.
[3] Alvar, "Ind. Lum.," sec. 25.   [4] *Ibid.*, sec. 21.
[5] *Ibid.*, sec. 53.
[6] See Koran, v. ad fin.:—"And when God shall say unto Jesus at the last day: O Jesus, son of Mary, hast thou said unto men, Take me and my mother for two Gods, beside God? he shall answer, Praise be unto thee! it is not for me to say that which I ought not."
[7] P. 56.

But the following extract from a treatise on Religions, by Ali ibn Hazm,[1] the prime minister of Abdurrahman V. (Dec. 1023-March 1024), will show that some educated Moslems knew enough of the Christian creed to appreciate its difficulties :—"We need not be astonished," says Ibn Hazm, "at the superstition of men. Look at the Christians ! They are so numerous that God only knows their numbers. They have among them men of great intelligence, and princes of great ability. Nevertheless they believe that three is one, and one is three ; that one of the three is the Father, another the Son, another the Spirit ; that the Father is, and is not, the Son ; that a man is, and is not, God ; that the Messiah is God in every respect, and yet not the same as God ; that He who has existed from all eternity has been created.

"One of their sects, the members of which they call Jacobites, and which number hundreds of thousands, believes even that the Creator Himself was scourged, crucified, and put to death ; so that the Universe for three days was deprived of its Governor."

Another extract from an Arabic writer will show us what the Moslems thought of the worship of St James, the patron saint of Spain, round whose shrine rallied the religious revival in the north of the Peninsula. It is Ibn Hayyan,[2] who, in his account of Almanzor's fiftieth expedition against the Christians, says :—"Shant Yakoh (Santiago)[3] is one of the sanctuaries most frequented, not only by the Christians of Andalus, but of the neighbouring continent, who look upon its church with a veneration such as Moslems entertain for the Caaba of Mecca ; for their Caaba is a colossal idol

---

[1] II. 227, apud Dozy, iii. 342. Ibn Hazm was, says Dozy, "a strict Moslem, *averse to judging divine questions by human reasoning.*"

[2] Al Makkari, ii. 293.

[3] Miss Yonge, p. 87, says the Arabs called him Sham Yakub, but what authority has this statement ?

(statue) which stands in the middle of the church. They swear by it, and repair to it in pilgrimage from the most distant parts, from Rome, as well as other countries beyond Rome, pretending that the tomb to be seen in the church is that of Yakob (James), one of the twelve apostles, and the most beloved by Isa (Jesus).—May the blessing of God be on him, and on our Prophet !—The Christians call this Yakob the brother of Jesus, because, while he lived, he was always with him. They say that he was Bishop of Jerusalem, and that he wandered over the earth preaching the religion [of Christ], and calling upon the inhabitants to embrace it, till he came to that remote corner of Andalus; that he then returned to Syria, where he died at the age of 120 solar years. They pretend likewise that, after the death of Yakob, his disciples carried his body and buried it in that church, as the most remote part, where he had left traces [of his preaching]."

In a country where literature and the arts were so keenly cultivated, as they were in Spain during the time of Arab domination, and where the rivalry of Christian, Jew, and Moslem produced a sustained period of intellectual activity such as the world has rarely seen, controversial theology could not fail to have been largely developed. But the books, if any were written, from the Christian or Moslem standpoint, have all perished, and we have only such slight and unsatisfactory notices left to us as those already quoted.

In estimating, therefore, what influences the rival religions of Spain had upon each other, we are driven to draw such inferences as we can from the meagre hints furnished to us by the writers of the period; from our knowledge of what Christianity was in Spain, and Mohammedanism in Africa, before they were brought into contact in Andalusia, compared with what they became after that contact had made itself felt; and from the observed effects of such relations elsewhere. Upon a careful consideration of these scattered

H

hints we shall see that certain effects were visible, which, had the amalgamation of the two peoples been allowed to continue uninterruptedly for a longer period, and had there been no disturbing element in the north of Spain and in Africa, would in all probability have led to some marked modification in one or both religions, and even to their nearer assimilation.

—— o ——

CHAPTER IX.

HERESIES IN SPAIN.

SUCH mixtures of religions are by no means without example in history. The Sabians, for instance, were the followers of a religion, which may have been a cross between Judaism, Christianity, and Magianism.[1] But Mohammedanism itself has furnished the most marked instances of such amalgamation. In Persia Islam combined with the creed of Zoroaster to produce Babyism; while in India Hinduism and Mohammedanism, fused together by the genius of Nanak Guru, have resulted in Sikhism.

It may be said that Mohammedanism has been able to unite with Zoroastrianism and Hinduism owing to their very dissimilarity with itself, whereas Christianity is too near akin to Islam to combine with it in such a way as to produce a religion like both, and yet different from either.[2] Christianity and Mohammedanism, each have two cardinal doctrines (and two only) which cannot be abrogated if they are to remain distinctive creeds. In one of these, the unity

[1] For an attempted compromise between Christianity and Brahmanism, see the proceedings of Beschi, a Roman Catholic priest, "Education and Missions," p. 14.   [2] Cp., however, the Druse religion.

of God, they agree. In the other they do, and always must, differ. The divinity of Christ on the one side, and the divine mission of Mohammed on the other, are totally incompatible doctrines. If the one is true, the other cannot be so. Surrender both, and the result is Judaism. No compromise would seem possible. Yet a compromise was attempted, if we can credit a statement attributed by Dozy to Ibn Khaldun,[1] in recounting the history of the successful rebel, Abdurrahman ibn Merwan ibn Yunas, who during the last quarter of the ninth century, while all Moslem Spain was a prey to the wildest anarchy, became a leader of the renegade or Muwallad party in Merida and the neighbourhood. Thinking to unite the Muwallads and Christians in one revolt, he preached to his countrymen a new religion, which held a place halfway between Christianity and Islam. This is all we are told of an endeavour, which might have led to the most important consequences. That we hear no more of it is evidence enough that the attempt proved abortive. The only other attempt, if it can be called so, to combine Islam and Christianity has resulted in that curious compound called the religion of the Druses.

But though no religion, holding a position midway between Islam and Christianity, arose in Spain, yet those religions could hardly fail to undergo considerable modifications in themselves by reason of their close contact for several centuries.

In respect to Christianity we shall naturally find the traces (if any) of such modification in the so-called heresies which may have arisen in Spain during this period. These will require a somewhat strict examination to be made to yield up their secret.

---

[1] Dozy, ii. 184. Dozy adds that Abdurrahman was called the Galician (el Jaliki) in consequence of this attempt of his : but there is some error here, as Ibn Hayyan (see Al Makkari, ii. 439, and De Gayangos' note) says he was called ibn ul'jaliki, *i.e.*, of the stock of the Galicians.

The Church of Spain seems to have gained a reputation for introducing innovations [1] into the doctrines and practices of the true faith, and even of priding itself on its ingenuity in this way. The very first Council whose acts have come down to us, held at Elvira in Spain, early in the fourth century, contains a canon censuring the use of pictures. The very first heretics, who were punished for their error with death by the hands of their fellow-Christians, were reared in the bosom of the Spanish Church. The doctrine, novel then, but accepted now by all the Western Churches, of the Procession of the Holy Ghost from the Son as well as from the Father, was first formulated in a Spanish Council at the end of the sixth century, but not universally received in the West until 600 years later.[2] And as we have seen, the use of pictures was denounced long before the times of the Iconoclasts.

We will now take in order the several heresies that made themselves noticeable in Spain, or Gothic Gaul, during the Arab supremacy, and see if we can trace any relation between them and the Moslem faith.

To take an unimportant one first, a heresy is mentioned as having arisen in Septimania (Gothic Gaul), presumably during the eighth century.[3] It was more practical than speculative, and consisted in a denial of the need of confession to a priest, on the (unimpeachable) ground that men ought to confess to God alone. This appears to us Protestants a wholly laudable and reasonable contention; but not so to the worthy abbé who records it : cette doctrine, *si*

---

[1] Alcuin ad Elipandum, iv. 13—"Audi me, obsecro, patienter, scholastica Hispaniae congregatio, tibi loquentem, quae novi semper aliquid audire vel praedicare desideras, non contenta ecclesiae universalis Catholica fide, nisi tu aliquid per te invenies, unde tuum nomen celebrares in mundo."   [2] Lateran Council, 1215.

[3] See, however, Alcuin's letter to the clergy of the province, Ep., 71. Migne, vol. ci. p. 1594.

favorable à libertinage, trouva un grand nombre de partisans, et excite encore le zèle d'Alcuin.[1]

That this error was due in any sense to the influence of the Arabs in the neighbouring territories of Spain, it is of course impossible to affirm, but at all events the reform was quite in the spirit of the verses of the Koran: "O ye who have received [2] the Scripture come to a just determination between us and you, that we worship not any except God, and associate no creature with Him: and that the one of us take not the other for lords, beside God." And "They take their priests and monks for their lords besides God." [3]

Let us next consider an heretical view of the Trinity attributed to Migetius (*circa* 750). According to the rather

[1] Rohrbacher, "Hist. Univ. dé l'Eglise Cathol.," ix. 309.

[2] Chap. iii. p. 39. See Sale's note: "that is, come to such terms of agreement as are indisputably consonant to the doctrine of all the prophets and Scriptures, and therefore cannot reasonably be rejected."

[3] Chap. ix. Mohammed charged the Jews and Christians with idolatry both on other grounds and because "they paid too implicit an obedience to their priests and monks, who took upon them to pronounce what things were lawful and what unlawful, and to dispense with the laws of God." See Sale, *Ibid.*

Cp.—

> Haughty of heart and brow the warrior came,
> In look and language proud as proud might be,
> Vaunting his lordship, lineage, fights, and fame,
> Yet was that barefoot monk more proud than he.
> And as the ivy climbs the tallest tree,
> So round the loftiest soul his toils he wound ;
> And with his spells subdued the fierce and free.
> Till ermined age and youth in arms renowned
> Honouring his scourge and hair-cloth meekly kissed the ground.
>
> And thus it chanced that valour, peerless knight,
> Who ne'er to king or kaiser veiled his crest,
> Victorious still in bull-feast or in fight,
> Since first with mail his limbs he did invest,
> Stooped ever to that anchoret's behest ;
> Nor reasoned of the right, nor of the wrong,
> But at his bidding laid the lance in rest,
> And wrought fell deeds the troubled world along,
> For he was fierce as brave, and pitiless as strong.
>
> —Scott's " Don Roderick," xxix. xxx.

obscure account, which has come down to us,[1] he seems to
have regarded the Three Persons of the Trinity, at least in
their relations with the world, as corporeal, the Father being
personified in David, the Son in Jesus, and the Holy Ghost
in Paul.   It is difficult to believe that the doctrine, thus
crudely stated by Elipandus, was really held by anyone.
We may perhaps infer[2] that Migetius revived the error of
Priscillian (itself a form of Sabellianism), and reducing the
Three Persons of the Trinity to one, acknowledged certain
ἐνεργείαι, or powers, emanating from Him, which were manifested in David, Jesus, Paul respectively.   As the first and
last of these three recipients of the Divine powers were
confessedly men, it follows that Migetius was ready to strip
Jesus of that Divinity, which is the cardinal doctrine of
Christianity, and which more than any other doctrine dis-
tinguishes it from the creed of Mohammed.   Accordingly
he appears to have actually denied the divinity of the
Word,[3] and in this he made an approach to Mohammedanism.[4]

A similar, but seemingly not identical, error was propagated by those who, as we learn from a letter of Alvar to
Speraindeo, did not believe the Three in One and One in
Three, "denying the utterances of the prophets, rejecting
the doctrine of learned men, and, while they claimed to
take their stand upon the Gospel, pointing to texts like
John xx. 17, 'I ascend unto my Father, and your Father,
unto my God and your God,' to prove that Christ was

---

[1] Elipandus to Migetius, sec. 3.   See Migne, vol. 96, p. 859.

[2] With Enhueber.   Dissert. apud Migne, ci., p. 338 ff., sec. 29.

[3] Enhueber, sec. 32.

[4] Neander, v. 216, n., says, Migetius held that the Λογος became personal with the assumption of Christ's humanity ; that the Λογος was the
power constituting the personality of Christ.   Hence, says Neander,
he was accused of asserting that Christ, the son of David according
to the flesh, and not Christ, the Son of God, was the Second Person of
the Trinity.

merely man." [1] In his answer to Alvar's letter, Speraindeo
says, " If we speak of the Trinity as one Person, we
Judaize ; " he might have added, "and Mohammedanize."
These heretics, according to the abbot, spoke of three
powers (*virtutes*) forming one Person, not, as the orthodox
held, three Persons forming one God.[2] Here we see a
close resemblance to the error mentioned in the preceding
paragraph ; but the heretics we are now dealing with make
an even closer approach to the teaching of Mohammed in
their quotation of John xx. 17 given above, as will be seen,
if we compare with that text the following passages of the
Koran, put into the mouth of Christ : " Verily, God is my
Lord, and your Lord ; therefore serve him : " [3] " They are
surely infidels who say, verily, God is Christ, the Son of
Mary, since Christ said, O children of Israel, serve God, my
Lord and your Lord : " [4] and, " I have not spoken unto
them any other than what thou didst command me—
namely, worship God, my Lord and your Lord." [5]

We come next to the famous Adoptionist heresy, the
most remarkable and original of those innovations to which
Alcuin taunts the Spanish Church with being addicted.
Unfortunately we derive little of our knowledge of the new
doctrine from the originators and supporters of it — our
information on the subject coming chiefly from passages
quoted by their opponents (notably our own Alcuin) in
controversial works. But that the heresy had an important
connection with the Mohammedan religion has been the

---

[1] Alvar's letter.   Florez, xi. 147.   Another text quoted in defence of
this doctrine of Agnoetism was Matt. xxiv. 36 : " Of that day and that
hour knoweth no man ; no, not the angels of heaven, but my Father
only."   In answer to this, Speraindeo refers to Gen. iii. 9, where God
the Father seems not to know where Adam is.

[2] Speraindeo's illustration of the Trinity cannot be called a happy
one.   He likens it to a king, whose power is one, but made up of the
man himself, his diadem, and his purple.

[3] Koran, c. iii. v. 46.   [4] Kor., c. v. 77.   [5] Kor., c. v. 118.

opinion of many eminent writers on Church history. Mariana, the Spanish historian, and Baronius, the apologist for the Roman Church, held that the object of the new heresiarchs was, "by lowering the character of Christ, to pave the way for a union between Christians and Mohammedans." [1]   Enhueber,[2] also, in his treatise on this subject, quotes a tract, "De Primatu Ecclesiae Toletanae," which attributes the heresy to its author, Elipandus, being brought into so close a contact with the Saracens, and living on such friendly terms with them.[3]

Neander [4] thinks that there are some grounds for supposing that Felix, one of the authors of the heresy, had been employed in defending Christianity against objections brought against it from the Moslem standpoint,[5] and in proving the divinity of Christ, so that they might be induced to accept it.   Felix, therefore, may have been led to embrace this particular doctrine, called Adoptionism, from a wish to bring the Christian view of Christ nearer to the Mohammedan opinion.

There is considerable doubt as to who first broached the new theory, the evidence being of a conflicting character, and pointing now to Elipandus, bishop of Toledo and primate of all Spain, now to Felix, bishop of Urgel, in Catalonia.[6]

[1] Mariana, vii. 8.   Baronius, "Ann. Eccl.," xiii. p. 260.   See Blunt, "Dictionary of Religions," etc., article on Adoptionism ; and Migne, vol. xcvi. p. 847—"deceptus uterque contagione forsan insidentium cervicibus aut e proximo blasphemantium Mohametanorum commercio."

[2] Enhueber, sec. 26.   Mansi, "Coll. Concil.," x. 513, sec. 4.

[3] "Usus enim frequenti Maurorum commercio."—*Ibid.*   [4] V. 219.

[5] This perhaps refers to a "disputatio cum sacerdote" which the Emperor Charles the Great had heard of as written by Felix.   Alcuin (see "Ep.," 85) knows nothing of it.   In his letter to Charles, Alcuin, speaking of a letter from Felix, says : "Inveni peiores errores, quam ante in eius scriptis legerem."

[6] The prevailing opinion seems to be that the new doctrine arose out of Elipandus' controversy with Migetius.

The claims of Felix [1] are supported by Eginhard,[2] Saxo, and Jonas of Orleans; while Paulinus of Aquileia, in his book entitled "Sacrosyllabus," expressly calls Elipandus the author of the baneful heresy; and Alcuin, in his letter to Leidrad,[3] says that he is convinced that Elipandus, as he was the first in rank, so also was the chief offender.

The evidence being inconclusive, we are driven to follow *à priori* considerations, and these point to Elipandus as the author. According to Neander,[4] he was a violent, excitable, bigoted man; and he certainly uses some very strong language in his writings against his opponents, and stands a good deal on his dignity as head of the Spanish Church. For instance, speaking of his accusers, Etherius, Bishop of Osma, and Beatus,[5] a priest of Libana, he says of the former that he wallows in the mire of all lasciviousness;[6] that he is totally unfit to officiate at God's altar;[7] that he is a false prophet [8] and a heretic; and, forgetting the courtesies of controversy, he doesn't hesitate, in another place, to call him an ass. Beatus also he accuses of gross sensuality, and calls him

[1] See "Froben Dissertation," Migne, vol. ci. p. 305.

[2] "Annals," 792,

[3] Alcuin, "Epist. ad Leidradum," says that the heresy arose in Cordova, and he appeals to Elipandus' letter to Felix after the latter's recantation.

[4] Neander (v. p. 217) seems to infer these qualities from his writings. An author, quoted by Enhueber (Tract. de Primata Eccl. Tolet), describes him as "parum accurate in sacris litteris versatus."

[5] Died in 798. Fleury v., p. 236.

[6] Elipand. Epist., iv. 2, "Carnis immunditia fetidus."

[7] "Ab altario Dei extraneus." Neander, v., p. 226, takes this to mean that he was deposed.

[8] He gave the Revelation of St John a Moslem application: and prophesied the end of the world in the near future. See letter of Beatus, book i., sec. 23—"Novissima hora est . . . nunc Antichristi multi facti sunt. Omnis spiritus qui solvit Jesum est illius Antichristi, quem audistis quoniam venit, et nunc in mundo est." See also Alcuin's letter to the Spanish bishops.

that iniquitous priest of Astorga,[1] accusing him of heresy, and giving him the title Antiphrasius, which means that instead of being called Beatus, he should have been named the very opposite.[2]

But in spite of outbreaks like these we must beware of judging the venerable Elipandus too hardly. Alcuin himself, in his letter to the bishop, written, as he says, " with the pen of charity," speaks of him as most blameless,[3] and confesses that he has heard much of his piety and devotion, an admission which he also makes with regard to Felix, in a letter to him.[4] Yet in his book against Elipandus, he exclaims, not without a touch of bathos: "For all the garments of wool on your shoulders, and the mitre upon your brow, wearing which you minister to the people, for all the daily shaving of your beard[5] . . . if you renounce not these doctrines, you will be numbered with the goats !" Another testimony (of doubtful value, however) in Elipandus' favour is to be found in the anonymous life of Beatus,[6] where Elipandus is said to have succeeded Cixila in the bishopric of Toledo, because of his reputation for learning and piety, which extended throughout Spain.

[1] " Elipandus and bishops of Spain to those of Gaul," sec. 1.

[2] This practice of punning on names is very common in these writers. "Infelix Felix " is a poor witticism which constantly occurs. So Samson says of Hostegesis that he ought to be called "'hostis Jesu " ; and in the account of the Translation of the bodies of Aurelius, etc., we find Leovigild spoken of as a very " Leo vigilans."

[3] " Sanctissime praesul," sec. 1. Cp. sec. 6, " Audiens famam bonam religiosae vitae de vobis."

[4] " Celeberriman tuae sanctitatis audiens famam." The "Pseudo Luit-prand " calls him " Vir humilis, prudens, ac in zelo fidei Catholicae fervens."

[5] Beards were the sign of laymen, see Alvar, " Ep.," xiii., and pro-bably the distinction was much insisted on because of the Moslem custom of wearing long beards. For the distinctive dress of the clergy see the same letter of Alvar, . . . " Quem staminia et lana ovium religiosum adprobat." [6] See Migne, xcvi., 890 ff.

Elipandus, who boasted of having refuted and stamped out the Migetian errors, and who also took up so independent an attitude with regard to the See of Rome, was not the man to endure being dictated to in the matter of what was, or what was not, sound doctrine, and, in the letter quoted above, he scornfully remarks that he had never heard that it was the province of the people of Libana to teach the Toledans. Here, as in the defiant attitude taken up towards the Pope, we may perhaps see a jealousy, felt by the old independent Church of Spain under its own primate, towards the new Church, that was growing up in the mountains of the North, the centre of whose religious devotion was soon to be Compostella, and its spiritual head not the primate of Spain, but the bishop of Rome.

It is now time to explain what the actual heresy advocated by Elipandus and Felix was. Some have held the opinion that Adoptionism was merely a revival of the Bonosian errors, which had long taken root in Spain;[1] others, that it was a revival of the Nestorian[2] heresy, a new phase of the controversy between the schools of Antioch and Alexandria;[3] or that it was an attempt to reform Christianity, purging it from later additions.[4] Alcuin, however, speaks of its followers as a new sect, unknown to former times.[5] Stated

---

[1] Enhueber, Diss., sec. 25. The errors of Bonosus were condemned at Capua in 389. For their development in Spain, see "Isidore of Seville."

[2] Condemned at Ephesus, 431. For connection of Adoptionism with this, see letter of Adrian to bishops of Spain (785?).

[3] Neander, v., p. 216.

[4] *Ibid.*, vi., p. 120, see letter of Alvar to Speraindeo.

[5] Alcuin contra Felicem, i., sec. 7. Elipandus denied that it had anything to do with other heresies. "Nos vero anathematizamus Bonosum, qui filium Dei sine matre genitum, adoptivum fuisse adfirmat. Item Sabellium, qui ipsum esse Patrem, quem Filium, quem et Spiritus sanctus (*sic*) et non ipsud, delirat. Anathematizamus Arium, qui Filium et Spiritum Sanctum creaturas esse existimat. Anathematizamus Manichaeum qui Christum solum Deum et non

briefly, the new doctrine was that Jesus, in so far as His manhood was concerned, was son of God by adoption. This error had been foreseen and condemned in advance by Cyril of Alexandria (348-386):[1] by Hilary of Arles (429-449).[2] The Eleventh Council of Toledo had also guarded against this same error a hundred years before this (675), affirming that Christ the Son of God was His Son by nature, not by adoption.

It is a mistake to suppose Adoptionism to be a mere resuscitation of Nestorianism.[3] It agreed with the latter in repudiating the term "Mother of God" as applied to the Virgin Mary,[4] but it differed from it in the essential point of acknowledging the unity of person in Christ. What Felix—and on him devolved the chief onus of defence in the controversy—wished to make clear, was that the predicates of Christ's two natures could not logically be interchanged.[5] He therefore reasoned thus : Christ in respect to His Deity is God, and Son of God ; with respect to His Manhood He is also God and Son of God, not indeed in essence, but by being taken into union with Him, who *is* in essence God, and Son of God. Therefore Christ, unless He derived His humanity from the essence of God, must as man, and in respect of that humanity, be Son of God only in a nuncupative sense. This relation of Jesus the Man to God he preferred to describe by the term Adoption—a word not found in Scripture in this connection, "but," says

---

hominem fuisse praedicat. Anathematizamus Antiphrasium Beatum carnis lasciviae deditum, et onagrum Etherium, doctorem bestialem . . .," etc.

[1] "Lectures on the Catechism," xi. "Christ is the Son of God by nature, begotten of the Father, not by adoption."

[2] De Trinit, v., p. 7, "The Son of God is not a false God—a God by adoption, or a God by metaphor (nec adoptivus, nec connuncupatus)."

[3] See Blunt, "Dict. of Relig.," article on Adoptionism.

[4] Neander, v. 223. Blunt (l.l.) says just the contrary.

[5] Neander, v. 220.

Felix, "implied therein,[1] for what is adoption in a son, if it be not election, assumption (*susceptio*)." The term itself was no doubt found by Elipandus in the Gothic Liturgy;[2] and he most likely used it at first with no thought of raising a metaphysical discussion on so knotty a point. Being brought to task, however, for using the word by those whom he deemed his ecclesiastical inferiors, he was led to defend it from a natural dislike to acknowledge himself in the wrong. "We can easily believe," says Enhueber, "that Elipandus, who appears to have been the chief author of the heresy at this time, fell into it at first from ignorance and inadvertently, and did not appear openly as a heretic, till, admonished of his error, he arrogantly and obstinately defended a position which he had only taken up through ignorance."[3]

Elipandus also seems to have applied to Felix[4] for his opinion on Christ's Sonship; and the latter, who was a man of great penetration and acuteness, first formulated the new doctrine, stating in his answer that Christ must be considered with regard to His Divinity as truly God and Son of God, but with regard to His Manhood, as Son of God in name only, and by adoption.

To give an idea of the lines on which the controversy was carried on, it will be necessary to state some of the arguments of Felix, and in certain cases Alcuin's rejoinders. These are :—

(*a.*) "If Christ, as man, is not the *adopted* Son of God,

---

[1] Alcuin contra Felicem, iii. c. 8.

[2] "Elipand. ad Albinum," sec. 11. Adoptio assumptio (ἀνάληψις) occurs (*a*) in the Missa de coena Domini : *adoptivi hominis passio ;* (*b*) in the prayer de tertia feria Pascha : *adoptionis gratia ;* (*c*) in that de Ascensione : *adoptionem carnis.* The Council of Frankfurt (794) branded the authors of the liturgy as heretics (so also did Alcuin) and as the main cause of the Saracen conquest ! See Fleury, v. 243.

[3] Enhueber, "Dissertatio," sec. 26. Neander, v. 217, has the same remark in other words.   [4] See Blunt, Art. on Adoptionism.

then must His Manhood be derived from the essence of God and consequently must be something different from the manhood of men."[1] To this Alcuin can only oppose another dilemma, which, however, is more of the nature of a quibble. "If," he says, "Christ is an adopted Son of God, and Christ is also God, then is God the adopted Son of God?"[2] Here Alcuin confounds the predicates of Christ's two natures—the very thing Felix protested against —and uses the argument thus obtained against that doctrine of Felix, which was based on this very denial of any interchange of predicates.

(*b.*) Christ is spoken of sometimes as Son of David, sometimes as Son of God. One person can only have two fathers, if one of these be an adoptive father. So is it with Christ. Alcuin answers: "As a man (body and soul) is called the son of his father, so Christ (God and man) is called Son of God."[3] But to those who deny that a man's soul is derived from his father, this argument would carry no weight.

(*c.*) Christ stood in a position of natural dependence towards God over and above the voluntary submission which He owed to His Father as God.[4] This dependence Felix expresses by the term *servus conditionalis*, applied to Jesus.[5] He may have been thinking of Matt. xii. 18, "Be-

---

[1] Alcuin contra Felicem, ii. sec. 12.

[2] Alcuin (*ibid.*, i. sec. 13) also answers: "If Christ be the adopted Son of God, because as man, he could not be of God's substance : then must he also be Mary's adopted son in respect to his Deity. But then Mary cannot be the mother of God." But this Alcuin thinks an impious conclusion. Cp. also Contra Felic., vii. sec. 2.

[3] Contra Felic., iii. sec. 2.

[4] Cp. 1 Corinth. xi. 3, "The Head of Christ is God." This position of dependence was due, says Felix, "ad ignobilitatem beatae Virginis, quae se ancillam Dei humili voce protestatur."

[5] Cp. Elipandus' "Confession of Faith": " . . . per istum Dei simul et hominis Filium, adoptivum humanitate et nequaquam adoptivum Divinitate . . . qui est Deus inter Deos (John x. 35) . . . quia,

hold my servant, whom I have chosen;" and St Paul's Ep. to Philipp. ii. 7, "He took upon Him the form of a servant, and was made in the likeness of men."[1] Or perhaps he had in his mind, if the theory of the influence of Mohammedanism is true, those passages of the Koran which speak of Christ as a servant, as, "Christ doth not proudly disdain to be a servant unto God,"[2] and, "Jesus is no other than a servant."[3]

(*d.*) To prove that Scripture recognises a distinction between Christ the Man and Christ the God, Felix appeals to Luke xviii. 19, "Why callest thou Me good? There is none good, save one, even God;" Mark xiii. 32, "Of that day, or that hour, knoweth no one, not even the angels in heaven, neither the Son, but the Father." Texts such as these can only be met by a reference to other texts, such as John iii. 16, where God is said to have given His only begotten Son to suffer death upon the Cross.

Conceiving, then, that it was logically necessary to speak of Christ the Man as Son of God by adoption, Felix yet admits that this adoption, though the same in kind[4] as that which enables *us* to cry Abba, Father, yet was more excellent in degree, and even perhaps specifically higher. It differed also from man's adoption in not being entered into at baptism, since Christ's baptism was only the point at which His adoption was outwardly made manifest by signs of miraculous power, which continued till the resurrection. Christ's adoption · according to Felix, was assumed at His conception, "His humanity developing in accordance with its own laws, but in union with the Logos."[5] It will be

---

si conformes sunt omnes sancti huic Filio Dei secundum gratiam, profecto et cum adoptione (sunt) adoptivi, et cum advocato advocati, et cum Christo Christi, et *cum servo servi.*"

[1] Cf. Acts iii. 13.   [2] Koran, iv. v. 170.   [3] Koran, xliii. v. 59.
[4] See John x. 35.   Cp. Neander, v. p. 222.
[5] Neander (l.l.)   Blunt, Art. on Adopt., puts this differently:
"There were (according to Felix) two births in our Lord's life—(*a*) the

seen that though Felix wished to keep clear the distinction between Christ as God, and as Man, yet he did not carry this separation so far as to acknowledge two persons in Christ. "The Adoptionists acknowledged the unity of Persons, but meant by this a juxtaposition of two distinct personal beings in such a way that the Son of God should be recognised as the vehicle for all predicates, but not in so close a manner as to amount to an absorption of the human personality into the Divine Person."[1] The two natures of Christ had been asserted by the Church against the Monophysites, and the two wills against the Monothelites, but the Church never went on to admit the two Persons.[2] With regard to the contention of Felix, we are consequently driven to the conclusion that either the personality ascribed to Christ was "a mere abstraction, a metaphysical link joining two essentially incompatible natures,"[3] or that the dispute was only about names, and that by adopted son Felix and the others meant nothing really different from the orthodox doctrine.[4]

The first mention of the new theory appears in a letter of Elipandus to the Abbot Fidelis, written in 783,[5] but it did

assumption of man at the conception ; (*b*) the adoption of that man at baptism. Cp. Contra Felic., iii. 16 : "Qui est Secundus Adam, accepit has geminas generationes ; primam quae secundum carnem est, secundum vero spiritatem, quae per adoptionem fit, idem redemptor noster secundum hominem complexus, in semet ipso continet, primam videlicet, quam suscepit ex virgine nascendo, secundam vero quam initiavit in lavacro [   ] a mortuis resurgendo."

[1] Blunt, article on Adopt.

[2] Cp. Paschasius : "In Christo gemina substantia, non gemina persona est, quia persona personam consumere potest, substantia vero substantiam non potest, siquidem persona res iuris est, substantia res naturae."

[3] Blunt, *ibid.* Cp. also Alcuin contra Felic., iv. 5, where he says that Felix, although he shrank from asserting the dual personality of Christ, yet insisted on points which involved it.

[4] So Walchius.   [5] See Migne, 96 p. 848.

not attract notice till a little later. The pope Adrian, in his letter to the orthodox bishops of Spain (785), speaks of the melancholy news of the heresy having reached him—a heresy, he remarks, never before propounded, unless by Nestorius. Together with Elipandus, he mentions Ascarius,[1] Bishop of Braga, whom Elipandus had won over to his views. The new doctrine seems to have made its way quickly over a great part of Spain,[2] while Felix propagated it with considerable success in Septimania. The champions of the orthodox party in Spain were Beatus and Etherius, whom we have mentioned above, and Theudula, Bishop of Seville; while beyond its borders Alcuin, Paulinus of Aquileia, and Agobard of Lyons, under the direction of Charles the Great and the Pope, defended the orthodox position.

Felix, being bishop in a province of which Charles claimed the overlordship, was amenable to his ecclesiastical superiors, and suffered for his opinions at their hands; but Elipandus, living under a Mohammedan government, could only be reached by letters or messages. He seems even to have received something more than a mere negative support from the Arabs, if we are right in so interpreting a passage in the letter of Beatus and Etherius.[3] But it is hard to believe that Elipandus was on such friendly terms with the Arab authorities; indeed, from passages in his writings, we should infer that the opposite was rather the

---

[1] Fleury, v. 236, mentions a letter of his to Elipandus, asking the latter's opinion on some doubtful points in the new doctrine.

[2] Jonas of Orleans, in his work against Claudius, says: "Hac virulenta doctrina uterque Hispaniam magna ex parte infecit."

[3] I. sec. 13. "Et episcopus metropolitanus et princeps terrae pari certamine schismata haereticorum, unus verbi gladio, alter virga regiminis ulciscens, de terra vestra funditus auferantur." See on this passage Neander, v. 227, and cp. sec. 65, "haereticus tamen scripturarum non facit rationem, sed cum potentibus saeculi ecclesiam vincere quaerit.

I

case.[1] Neander suggests that it may have been a Gothic king in Galicia who supported Elipandus, but this seems even more unlikely than the other supposition.

The first council called to consider this question was held by the suggestion of the Emperor and the Pope at Narbonne in 788, when the heresy was condemned by twenty-five bishops of Gaul.[2]

A similar provincial council was held by Paulinus at Friuli in 791, with the same results.[3] But in the following year the heresy was formally condemned at a full council held at Ratisbon, under the presidency of the Emperor. Here Felix abjured his error, and was sent to Rome to be further condemned by the Pope, that the whole Western Church might take action in the matter. Felix was there induced to write a book condemning his own errors, but in spite of this he was not restored to his see.[4] On his return, however, to Spain, Felix relapsed into his old heresy, which he had never really abjured.[5]

In 792 Alcuin was summoned from England to come and defend the orthodox position. He wrote at once to Felix a kindly letter, admonishing him of his errors, and acknowledging that all his previous utterances on theology had been sound and true. Felix answered this letter, but his reply is not preserved. To the same, or following, year belongs the letter of Elipandus and the bishops of Spain to

---

[1] Elip. ad. Albinum, sec. 7—"Oppressione gentis afflicti non possumus tibi rescribere cuncta;" also, Ad Felic. "quotidiana dispendia quibus duramus potius quam vivimus."

[2] There are some doubts about this council.

[3] Fleury, v. 236. Hefele dates it 796.

[4] See letter of Spanish bishops to Charles, asking for Felix's restoration (794).

[5] Leo III. said of him, at a council held in Rome (799): "*Fugiens ad paganos consentaneos* perjuratus effectus est.   See Froben, "Dissert," sec. 24; apud Migne, ci., pp. 305-336.

Charles and the bishops of Gaul, defending their doctrine, and asking for the restoration of Felix.

In 794 was held another council at Frankfurt, at which Alcuin and other English clergy were present. Felix was summoned to attend, and heard his heresy again condemned and anathematised, the decree to this effect being sent to Elipandus.[1] Alcuin's book was read by Charles, and sent into Septimania by the hands of the abbot Benedict.

The next council was held at Rome in 798 to confirm the one at Frankfurt.[2] In 799 came out Felix's answer to Alcuin, sent by him first to Elipandus, and, after being shewn to the Cordovan clergy, sent on to Charles. Alcuin is charged to answer it, with Paulinus and the Pope as his coadjutors.

In the same year another council was held at Aix, where Alcuin argued for a week with Felix, and apparently convinced him, for Felix again recanted, and even wrote a confession of faith discarding the word adoption, but still preserving the distinction of predicates belonging to the two natures.[3] Alcuin's book, after being revised by Charles, was published 800 A.D. Previously to this he had written to Elipandus, who answered in no measured terms, accusing Alcuin, among other things, of enormous wealth. This letter was sent through Felix, and, in answer, Alcuin wrote the book against Elipandus, which we now have, and which was the means of converting twenty thousand heretics in Gothic Gaul.[4] But in spite of Emperor or Pope, of the books of Alcuin, or the anathemas of the councils, neither Felix nor Elipandus really gave up his new doctrines, and

---

[1] Fleury, v. 243, says there was no anathema; but Migne, xcvi. 858, gives us the canon: "Anathematizata esto impia ac nefanda haeresis Elipandi Toletanae sedis Episcopi, et Felix (*sic*) Orgellitani, eorumque sequacium."

[2] Neander, v. 228. 　　　　　　　　　　[3] *Ibid.*, p. 232.

[4] Froben, sec. 82. Neander says 10,000.

even the former continued to make converts. Elipandus, though very old [1] at this time (800 A.D.), lived ten years longer, and Felix survived him eight years;[2] and they both died persisting in their error.[3]

We have dealt somewhat at length with the Adoptionist heresy, both from its interest and importance, and because, as mentioned above, there are some reasons for thinking that it was the outcome of a wish to conciliate Mohammedan opinion. It will be as well to recapitulate such evidence as we have obtained on this point. But we must not expect to find the traces of Mohammedan influence in the development, so much as in the origination, of the theory. What we do find is slight enough, amounting to no more than this :—

(*a.*) That the one point, which repelled the Mohammedan from genuine Christianity—setting aside for a moment the transcendental mystery of the Trinity—was the Divinity of Christ. Anything, therefore, that tended to emphasise the humanity of Jesus, or to obscure the great fact of Christ the Man, being Son of God, which sounded so offensive to Mohammedan ears, would so far bring the Christian creed nearer to the Mohammedan's acceptance, by assimilating the Christian conception of Christ, to that which appears so often in the Koran.[4] There can be no doubt that the theory

---

[1] Alcuin adv. Elip. Preface to Leidrad : " Non pro eius tantum-modo laboravi salute, quem timeo forsan citius vel morte praereptum esse propter decrepitam in eo senectutem."   [2] Or perhaps six.

[3] No reliance can be placed in the statement of the Pseudo-Luitprand, who, in a letter to Recemundus, speaking of Elipandus, says : " Post-quam illius erroris sui de adoptione Christi sero et vere poenituit, ad quod manifestandum concilium (795) episcoporum . . . collegit ; et coram omnibus abiurato publice errore *fidem sanctae ecclesiae Romanae* confessus est." These words in italics reveal a later hand. Cp. also sec. 259 and Julianus. Alcuin, in a letter to Aquila, bishop of Salis-bury, says that Elipandus in 800 A.D. still adhered to his error.

[4] Fifty years later Alvar (" Ind. Lum.," sec. 9), accuses certain

of adoption, if carried to its logical conclusion, did contribute to this result:

(*b.*) That Elipandus was accused of receiving the help of the secular arm in disseminating his heretical opinions:

(*c.*) That the application of the term *Servant* to Christ, besides being authorised by texts from Scripture, is countenanced in two passages from the Koran:

(*d.*) That Leo III., speaking of Felix's return to Spain, and his relapse into error, implies that it was due to his renewed contact with infidels who held similar views:

(*e.*) That in a passage, quoted by Enhueber, Elipandus is said to have lost his hold on the truth in consequence of his close intercourse with the Arabs:

(*f.*) That Elipandus accused Etherius of being a false prophet, that is, for giving, as has been conjectured, a Mohammedan interpretation to the Beast in the Revelation of St John.

Something must now be said of one more doctrine, which, though it did not arise in Spain, nor perhaps much affected it, yet was originated by a Spaniard, and a disciple of Felix,[1]—Claudius, Bishop of Turin. Some have seen in this doctrine, which was an offshoot of Iconoclasm, traces of Adoptionism, a thing not unlikely in itself.[2]

Of the relations of Claudius to the Saracens we have the direct statement of one of his opponents, who said that the Jews praised him, and called him the wisest among the Christians; and that he on his side highly commended them *and the Saracens.*[3] Yet his tendency seems to have been against the Judaizing of the Church.[4]

Christians of dissembling their religion under fear of persecution :—
" Deum Christum non aperte coram eis (*i.e.* Saracenis) sed fugatis sermonibus proferunt, Verbum Dei et Spiritum, ut illi asserunt, profitentes, suasque confessiones corde, quasi Deo omnia inspiciente, servantes."

[1] Jonas of Orleans (Migne, cvi. p. 330) calls him so, and says elsewhere, " Felix resuscitur in Claudio."

[2] Neander, vi. 119.   [3] Fleury, v. 398.   [4] Neander, vi. 125.

The great Iconoclastic reform, which arose in the East, undoubtedly received its originating impulse from the Moslems. In 719 the Khalif destroyed all images in Syria. His example was followed in 730 by the Eastern Emperor, Leo the Isaurian. He is said to have been persuaded to this measure by a man named Bezer, who had been some years in captivity among the Saracens.[1] In 754 the great council of Constantinople condemned images. Unfortunately neither the great patriarchates nor the Pope were represented, and so this council never obtained the sanction of all Christendom ; and its decrees were reversed in 787 at the Council of Nicæa. In 790 appeared the Libri Carolini, in which we rejoice to find our English Alcuin helping Charles the Great to make a powerful and reasonable protest against the worship of images.[2] In 794 this protest was upheld by the German Council of Frankfurt. But the Pope, and his militia,[3] the monks, made a strenuous opposition to any reform in this quarter, and the recognition of images became part and parcel of Roman Catholic Christianity.

Claudius was made bishop of Turin in 828.[4] Though placed over an Italian diocese, he soon shewed the independence, which he had imbibed in the free air of Spain, where the Mohammedan supremacy had at least the advantage of making the supremacy of the Pope impossible. Finding that the people of his diocese paid worship to their

---

[1] Fleury, xl. ii. 1, says he was an apostate. See Mendham, Seventh General Council, Introd., pp. xii. xiv.

[2] "Adorationem soli Deo debitam imaginibus impertire aut segnitiae est, si utcumque agitur, aut insaniae, vel potius infidelitatis, si pertinaciter defenditur."—III. c. 24.

"Imagines vero, omni cultura et adoratione seclusa, utrum in basilicis propter memoriam rerum gestarum sint, nullum fidei Catholicae afferre poterunt praeiudicium, quippe cum ad peragenda nostrae salutis mysteria nullum penitus officium habere noscantur."—III. c. 21.

[3] Prescott.   [4] Neander says 814, Herzog 820.

images, Claudius set to work to deface, burn, and abolish, all images and crosses in his bishopric. In respect to the crosses he went further than other Iconoclasts, in which we can perhaps trace his Adoptionist training.[1]

These new views did not, as might be expected, find favour with the Catholic party, whose cause was taken up by Theodemir, abbot of Nîmes, a friend of Claudius', by Jonas of Orleans, and Dungal, an Irish priest. But, as in the case of Felix, the heresiarch was more than a match for his opponents in argument.[2]

Claudius' own defence has been lost, but we gather his views from his opponents' quotation of them.

Briefly expressed, they are as follows :—

(*a.*) Image-worship is really idol-worship :

(*b.*) If images are to be adored, much more should those living beings be adored, whom the images represent. But we are not permitted to adore God's works, much less may we worship the work of men :[3]

(*c.*) The cross has no claim to be adored, because Jesus was fastened to it : else must we adore other things with which Jesus was similarly connected ; virgins, for example, for Christ was nine months in a virgin's womb ; mangers, asses, ships, thorns, for with all these Jesus was connected. To adore the cross we have never been told, but to bear it,[4] that is to deny ourselves. Those generally are the readiest

---

[1] Neander, v. 119. The Spanish Christians were not free from the charge of adoring the cross, as we can see from the answer of the Khalif Abdallah (888) when advised to leave his brother's body at Bobastro : shall I, he said, leave my brother's body to the mercy of those who ring bells and adore the cross. Ibn Hayyan, apud Al Makk., ii. 446.

[2] Fleury, v. 398, confesses that the case of the image-worshippers rests mainly on tradition and the usage of the Church—meaning that they can draw no support from the Bible. He might have remembered Matt. xv. 7—"Ye make void the Word of God because of your tradition."

[3] Jonas of Orleans, apud Migne, vol. cvi. p. 326.   [4] Luke xiv. 27.

to adore it, who are least ready to bear it either spiritually or physically.[1]

Claudius also had very independent views on the question of papal supremacy.[2] Being summoned before a council, with more wisdom than Felix, he refused to attend it, knowing that his cause would be prejudged, and contented himself with calling the proposed assembly a congregation of asses.   He died in 839 in secure possession of his see, and with his Iconoclastic belief unshaken.

Such were the heresies which connect themselves with Spain during the first three hundred years of Arab domination, and which seem to have been, in part at least, due to Mohammedan influence. One more there was, the Albigensian heresy, which broke out one hundred and fifty years later, and was perhaps the outcome of intercourse with the Mohammedanism of Spain.[3]

----0----

CHAPTER X.

SOCIAL INFLUENCE OF CHRISTIANITY.

HAVING considered the effects of Mohammedanism on doctrinal Christianity (there are no traces of similar effects on doctrinal Mohammedanism), it will fall within the scope of our inquiry to estimate the extent to which those influences were reciprocally felt by the two religions in their social and intellectual aspects ; and how far the character of a Christian or a Mohammedan was altered by contact with a people professing a creed so like, and yet

---

[1] Jonas, apud Migne, vol. cvi. p. 351.

[2] See Appendix B, pp. 161-173.

[3] So Blunt.   It found followers in Leon.   See Mariana, xii. 2, from Lucas of Tuy.

so unlike.[1]   This influence we shall find more strongly manifested in the action of Christianity on Islam, than the reverse.

It is well known that Mohammed, though his opinion as to monks seems to have varied[2] from time to time, is reported to have expressly declared that he would have no monks in his religion.[3]   Abubeker, his successor,—if Gibbon's translation may be trusted,—in his marching orders to the army, told them to let monks and their monasteries alone.[4]   It was not long, however, before an order of itinerant monks—the faquirs—arose among the Moslems.   In other parts of their dominions these became a recognised, and in some ways privileged, class; but in Andalusia they did not receive much encouragement,[5] though they were very numerous even there.   Most of them, says the Arabian historian,[6] were nothing more than beggars, able but unwilling to work.   This remark, however, he tells us, must not be applied to all, "for there were among them men who, moved by sentiments of piety and devotion, left the world and its vanities, and either retired to convents to pass the remainder of their days among brethren of the same community, or putting on the dar-

---

[1] Mohammedanism is even called a *heresy* by a writer quoted by Prescott, "Ferdin. and Isab.," p. 244.

[2] Kor. v. 85—"Thou shalt find those to be most inclinable to entertain friendship for the true believers who say, We are Christians. This comes to pass, because there are priests and monks among them." Kor. lvii. 27—"As to the monastic state (Deus loquitur), the Christians instituted the same (we did not prescribe it for them) only out of desire to please God, yet they observed not the same as it ought truly to be observed." See also Kor. ix. 34—"Verily many of the priests and monks devour the substance of men in vanity, and obstruct the way of God ;" and Kor. xxiii. 55.

[3] Kor. v. 89. Sale's note.

[4] So Almanzor spared the monk of Compostella. Al Makkari, ii. 209.   [5] See the interesting account, *ibid.*, i. 114.

[6] Al Makkari.

wázah, and grasping the faquir's staff, went through the
country begging a scanty pittance, and moving the faithful
to compassion by their wretched and revolting appearance."
That Moslem monkeries did exist, especially in rather later
times, we can gather from the above passage and from
another place,[1] where a convent called Zawiyatu l'Mahruk
(the convent of the burnt) is mentioned.   On that passage
De Gayangos[2] has an interesting note, in which he quotes
from an African writer an account of a monastic establishment near Malaga.[3]   The writer says : " I saw on a moun-
tain, close to this city, a convent, which was the residence
of several religious men living in community, and conver-
sant with the principles of Sufism : they have a superior to
preside over them, and one or more servants to attend to
their wants.   Their internal regulations are really admirable ; each faquir lives separately in a cell of his own, and
meets his comrades only at meals or prayers.   Every morning at daybreak the servants of the community go round to
each faquir, and inquire of him what provisions he wishes
to have for his daily consumption. . . . They are served
with two meals a day.   Their dress consists of a coarse
woollen frock, two being allowed yearly for each man—one
for winter, another for summer.   Each faquir is furnished
likewise with a regular allowance of sugar, soap to wash his
clothes, oil for his lamp, and a small sum of money to
attend the bath, all these articles being distributed to them
every Friday. . . . Most of the faquirs are bachelors, a few
only being married.   These live with their wives in a
separate part of the building, but are subject to the same
rule, which consists in attending the five daily prayers,
sleeping at the convent, and meeting together in a lofty-
vaulted chamber, where they perform certain devotions.
. . . In the morning each faquir takes his Koran and reads

---

[1] Al Makkari, i. 115.   [2] *Ibid.*, i. p. 406, note.
[3] In the fourteenth century.

the first chapter, and then that of the king ; [1] and when the reading is over, a Koran, previously divided into sections, is brought in for each man to read in turn, until the whole is completed. On Fridays and other festivals these faquirs are obliged to go to the mosque in a body, preceded by their superior. . . . They are often visited by guests, whom they entertain for a long time, supplying them with food and other necessaries. The formalities observed with them are as follows :—If a stranger present himself at the door of the convent in the garb of a faquir, namely, with a girdle round his waist, his kneeling-mat suspended between his shoulders, his staff in his right hand, and his drinking vessel in his left, the porter of the convent comes up to him immediately, and asks what country he comes from, what convent he has resided in, or entered on the road, who was the superior of it, and other particulars, to ascertain that the visitor is not an impostor. . . . This convent was plentifully endowed with rents for the support of its inmates, for besides the considerable revenue in lands which was provided by its founder, a wealthy citizen of Malaga, who had been governor of the city under the Almohades, pious men are continually adding to the funds either by bequests in land or by donations in money."

The resemblance between these faquirs and Christian monks is sufficiently obvious, and need not be dilated upon : and though this particular convent was established at a later time, we cannot doubt that the influence, which produced such a modification of the very spirit of Islam, must have made itself felt much earlier. This is apparent in the analogous case of Moslem nuns, as a passage from an Arab writer seems to shew,[2] where it is said that the body of the Moorish king, Gehwar (1030-1043), was followed to the grave even by the damsels who had retired into solitude.

[1] ? Chapter 67.
[2] Conde, ii. 154. Unless the writer is referring to Christian nuns.

But over and above copying the institutions of Christianity, Islam shews signs of having become to a certain extent pervaded with a Christian spirit. It is easy to be mistaken in such things, but the following anecdotes are more in keeping with the Bible than the Koran. Hischem I. (788-796) in his last words to his son, Hakem I., said: "Consider well that all empire is in the hand of God, who bestoweth it on whom He will, and from whom He will He taketh it away.[1] But since God hath given to us the royal authority and power, which is in our hands by His goodness only, let us obey His holy will, which is no other than that we do good to all men,[2] and in especial to those placed under our protection. See thou therefore, O my son, that thou distribute equal justice to rich and poor, nor permit that any wrong or oppression be committed in thy kingdom, for by injustice is the road to perdition. Be clement, and do right to all who depend upon thee, for all are the creatures of God."[3]

The son was not inferior to the father, and capable, as the following story shews, of the most Christian generosity.[4] One of the faquirs who had rebelled against Hakem being captured and brought into the presence of the king, did not shrink in his bigotry and hate from telling the Sultan that in hating him he was obeying God. Hakem answered: "He who bid thee, as thou sayest, hate me, bids me pardon thee. Go, and live in God's protection."[5]

Prone as the Mohammedans were to superstition, and many as are the miracles and wonders, which are described in their histories, it must be acknowledged that their

---

[1] Daniel, iv. 25, and Koran, ii. v. 249—"God giveth His kingdom unto whom He pleaseth;" and Koran, iii. v. 24.

[2] Galatians vi. 20—"Let us do good unto all men, especially unto them that are of the household of faith." [3] Conde, i. 240.

[4] It is fair to state that Hakem I. was not always so generous.

[5] Lane-Poole, "Story of the Moors," p. 77.

capacity for imagining and believing in miracles never equalled that of Christian priests in the Middle Ages.[1]

We hear indeed of a vision of Mohammed appearing to Tarik, the invader of Spain;[2] of a miraculous spring gushing forth at the prayer of Akbar ibn Nafir;[3] of the marvellous cap of Omar;[4] of the wonders that distinguished the corpse of the murdered Hosein; of the vision shewing the tomb of Abu Ayub;[5] but nothing that will bear a comparison with the invention of St James' body at Ira Flavia (Padron), nor the clumsy and unblushing forgery of relics at Granada in the year of the Armada.[6] Yet the following story of Baki ibn Mokhlid, from Al Kusheyri,[7] reminds us forcibly of similar monkish extravagancies. A woman came to Baki, and said that, her son being a prisoner in the hands of the Franks, she intended to sell her house and go in search of him; but before doing so she asked his advice. Leaving her for a moment he requested her to wait for his answer. He then went out and prayed fervently for her son's release, and telling the mother what he had done, dismissed her. Some time after the mother came back with her son to thank Baki for his pious interference, which had procured her son's release. The son then told his story :—
"I was the king's slave, and used to go out daily with my brother slaves to certain works on which we were employed. One day, as we were going I felt all of a sudden as if my

---

[1] See the story of Atahulphus, Bishop of Compostella, and the bull —Alfonso of Burgos, ch. 66 : a man swallowed up by the earth—Mariana, viii. 4 : Sancho the Great's arm withered and restored—*Ibid.*, c. 10 : a Sabellian heretic carried off by the devil in sight of a large congregation—Isidore of Beja, sec. 69 : the miracle of the roses (1050)— Mar. ix. 3.   [2] Cardonne, i. p. 72.   [3] *Ibid*, p. 38.   [4] See Ockley.

[5] Gibbon, "for such are the manufacture of every religion," p. 115.

[6] See Geddes, Miscell. Tracts, "an account of MSS. and relics found at Granada." But we must remember that these miraculous phenomena appear much earlier in the history of Islam than of Christianity.

[7] Al Makkari, ii. 129 ; cp. Conde, i. 355.

fetters were being knocked off. I looked down to my feet, when lo! I saw the heavy irons fall down broken on each side." The inspector naturally charged him with trying to escape, but he denied on oath, saying that his fetters had fallen off without his knowing how. They were then riveted on again with additional nails, but again fell off. The youth goes on :—" The Christians then consulted their priests on the miraculous occurrence, and one of them came to me and inquired whether I had a father. I said ' No, but I have a mother.' Well, then, said the priest to the Christians, ' God, no doubt, has listened to her prayers. Set him at liberty,' " which was immediately done. As a set-off to this there is a remarkable instance of freedom from superstition recorded of King Almundhir (881-2).[1] On the occasion of an earthquake, the people being greatly alarmed, and looking upon it as a direct interposition of God, this enlightened prince did his best to convince them that such things were natural phenomena, and had no relation to the good or evil that men did,[2] shewing that the earth trembled for Christian and Moslem alike, for the most innocent as well as the most injurious of creatures without distinction. They, however, refused to be convinced.

This independence of thought in Almundhir was perhaps an outcome of that philosophic spirit which first shewed itself in Spain in the reign of this Sultan's predecessor.[3] The philosophizers were looked upon with horror by the theologians, who worked upon the people, so that at times they were ready to stone and burn the free-thinkers.[4] The works of Ibnu Massara, a prominent member of this school, were burnt publicly at Cordova ;[5] and the great Almanzor, though himself, like the great Cæsar, indifferent to such

---

[1] Conde, i. 317. [2] Cp. Matt. v. 45 : Luke xiii. 4. [3] Dozy, iii. 18.
[4] Al Makk., i. 136, 141. They were called Zendik or heretics by the pious Moslems. See also Said of Toledo, apud Dozy, iii. 109.
[5] Al Makk., ii. 121.

questions,[1] by way of gaining the support of the masses, was ready, or pretended to be ready, to execute one of these philosophers.   At length, with feigned reluctance, he granted the man's life at the request of a learned faqui.[2]

Even among the Mohammedan " clergy "—if the term be allowable—there were Sceptics and Deists,[3] and others who followed the wild speculations of Greek philosophy.   Among the last of these, the greatest name was Averroes, or more correctly, Abu Walid ibn Roshd (1126-1198), who besides holding peculiar views about the human soul that would almost constitute him a Pantheist, taught that religion was not a branch of knowledge that could be systematised, but an inward personal power :[4] that science and religion could not be fused together.   Owing to his freedom of thought he was banished to a place near Cordova by Yusuf abu Yakub in 1196.   He was also persecuted and put into prison by Abdulmumen, son of Almansur,[5] for studying natural philosophy.   Another votary of the same forbidden science, Ibn Habib, was put to death by the same king.

Side by side with, and in bitter hostility to, the earlier freethinkers lived the faquis or theologians.   The Andalusians originally belonged to the Mohammedan sect of Al Auzai[6] (711-774), whose doctrines were brought into Spain by the Syrian Arabs of Damascus.   But Hischem I., on coming to

---

[1] He was supposed to be in secret addicted to the forbidden study of Natural Science and Astrology.—Al Makk., i. 141.   Yet he let the faquis make an "index expurgatorius" of books to be burnt.— Dozy, iii. 115.   His namesake, Yakub Almansur (1184-1199), ordered all books on Logic and Philosophy to be burnt.

[2] Dozy, iii. 261.   [3] Dozy, iii. 262, 263.

[4] See article in the "Encyclop. Britann."

[5] Al Makk., i. 198.   De Gayangos, in a note, points out that this was a mistake : for Abdulmumen was grandfather of Yakub Almansur, and could not be the king meant here.   He therefore reads, " Yakub, one of the Beni Abdulmumen."

[6] Al Makk., i. 403.   De Gayangos' note.

the throne, shewed his preference for the doctrines of Malik ibn Aus,[1] and contrived that they should supplant the dogmas of Al Auzai.   It may be that Hischem I. only shewed a leaning towards Malik's creed, without persuading others to conform to his views, but at all events the change was fully accomplished in the reign of his successor, Hakem I., by the instrumentality of Yahya ibn Yahya Al Seythi, Abu Merwan Abdulmalek ibn Habib,[2] and Abdallah Zeyad ibn Abdurrahman Allakhmi, three notable theologians of that reign.   Yahya returned from a pilgrimage to the East in 827, and immediately took the lead in the opposition offered to Hakem I. on the ground of his being a lax Mussulman, but, in reality, because he would not give the faquis enough power in the State.[3]

In the reign of Mohammed (852) these faquis had become powerful enough to impeach the orthodoxy of a well-known devout Mussulman, Abu Abdurrahman ibn Mokhli, but the Sultan, with a wise discretion, as commendable as it was rare, declared that the distinctions of the Ulema were cavils, and that the expositions of the new traditionist "conveyed much useful instruction, and inculcated very laudable practices."[4]

Efforts were made from time to time to overthrow this priestly ascendency, as notably by Ghazali, the "Vivificator," as he was called, " of religious knowledge."   This attempt failed, and the rebel against authority was excommunicated.[5] Yet the strictly oxthodox party did not succeed in arresting — to any appreciable extent — the progress of the decay which was threatening to attack even the distinctive

---

[1] Died 780.   Al Makk., i. 113, 343, ascribes the change to Hakem I.; and an author quoted, i. p. 403, ascribes it to Abdurrahman I.

[2] Al Makk., ii. 123.

[3] Al Makk., i. 113, implies the reverse of this.   Dozy, ii. p. 59.

[4] Conde, i. 294.   [5] Dozy, iv. 255.

features of the Mohammedan religion.[1] It is a slight indication of this, that the peculiar Moslem dress gradually began
to be given up, and the turban was only worn by faquis,[2]
and even they could not induce the people to return to a
habit once thought of great importance.[3]

But in other and more important respects we can see the
disintegrating effect which intercourse with Christians had
upon the social institutions of the Koran.[4]

(*a*.) Wine, which is expressly forbidden by Mohammed,[5]
was much drunk throughout the country,[6] the example
being often set by the king himself. Hakem I. seems to
have been the first of these to drink the forbidden juice.[7]
His namesake, Hakem II. (961-976), however, set his face
against the practice of drinking wine, and even gave orders
for all the vines in his kingdom to be rooted up—an edict
which he recalled at the instance of his councillors, who
pointed out that it would ruin many poor families, and
would not cure the evil, as wine would be smuggled in or
illicitly made of figs or other fruit. Hakem consequently
contented himself with forbidding anew the use of spiritu-
ous liquors in the most stringent terms.[8] Even the faquis
had taken to drinking wine, and they defended the practice
by saying that the prohibition might be disregarded by

---

[1] In spite of Al Makkari's statement, i. 112, where he says that all
innovations and heretical practices were abhorred by the people. If
the Khalif, he says, had countenanced any such, he would have been
torn to pieces. [2] Dozy, iii. 271. [3] Al Makkari, ii. 109.

[4] Al Makkari, ii., App. 28. Author quoted by De Gayangos:
The Moslems in the eleventh century "began to drink wine and
commit all manner of excesses. The rulers of Andalus thought of
nothing else than purchasing singing-women and slaves, listening to
their music, and passing the time in revelry and mirth."

[5] Kor. v. 93—"Surely wine, lots, and images are an abomination of
the work of Satan . . . avoid them."

[6] Al Makkari, ii. p. 171. [7] Cardonne, i. p. 252.

[8] Al Makkari, i. p. 108; ii. p. 171.

Moslems, who were engaged in a perpetual war with infidels.

(*b.*) Music was much cultivated, yet a traditionary saying of Mohammed runs thus : " To hear music is to sin against the law ; to perform music is to sin against religion ; to enjoy music is to be guilty of infidelity." [1] Abdurrahman II. (822-852) in especial was very fond of music, and gave the great musician Ziryab or Ali ibn Nafi a home at his Court, when the latter was driven from the East by professional jealousy.   Strict Mohammedans always protested against these violations of their law.   The important sect of Han-balites in particular, like our own Puritans, made a crusade against these abuses.   They "caused a great commotion in the tenth century in Baghdad by entering people's houses and spilling their wine, if they found any, and beating the singing-girls they met with and breaking their instruments." [2]

(*c.*) The wearing of silk, which had been disapproved of by Mohammed, became quite common among the richer classes, though the majority do not seem to have indulged themselves in this way.[3]

(*d.*) The prohibition of sculptures, representing living creatures, was disregarded.   We find a statue, raised to Abdurrahman's wife Zahra, in the Medinatu'l Zahra, a palace built by Abdurrahman III. in honour of his beloved mistress.   Images of animals are mentioned on the foun-tains,[4] and a .lion on the aqueduct.[5]   We also hear of a statue at the gate of Cordova.[6]

(*e.*) The Spanish Arabs even seem to have given up turning towards Mecca : for what else can we infer from a

---

[1] Yonge, "Moors in Spain," p. 71.

[2] Sale, Koran, Introduc., p. 122. (Chandos Classics.)

[3] Al Makkari, ii. p. 109.   In 678 Yezid, son of Muawiyah, was objected to as a drunkard, a lover of music, and a wearer of silk.   See Ockley, p. 358. (Chandos Classics.)   [4] Al Makkari, i. p. 236.

[5] *Ibid.*, p. 241.   [6] Akbar Madjmoua. Dozy, ii. p. 272.

fact mentioned by an Arab historian,[1] that Abu Obeydah was called Sahibu l'Kiblah as a distinctive nickname, because he did so turn?

(*f.*) A reformer seems even to have arisen, who wished to persuade his coreligionists to eat the flesh of sows, though not of pigs or boars.[2]

There is good reason to suppose that all this relaxation of the more unreasonable prohibitions of the Koran was due to contact with a civilised and Christian nation, partly in subjection to the Arabs, and partly growing up independently side by side with them. But in nothing was this shewn more clearly than in the social enfranchisement of the Moslem women, whom it is the very essence of Mohammed's teaching to regard rather as the goods and chattels than as the equals of man ; and also in the introduction among the Moslems of a more Christian conception of the sacred word—Love.

Consequently we become accustomed to the strange spectacle — strange among a Mohammedan people — of women making a mark in the society of men, and being regarded as intellectually and socially their equals. Thus we hear of an Arabian Sappho, Muatammud ibn Abbad Volada, daughter of Almustakfi Billah ;[3] of Aysha, daughter of Ahmad of Cordova—"the purest, loveliest, and most learned maiden of her day ;"[4] of Mozna, the slave and private secretary of Abdurrahman III.[5]

Again, contrary to the invariable practice elsewhere, women were admitted into the mosques in Spain. This

---

[1] Al Makkari, i. 149.

[2] Hamim, a Berber, in 936. He was crucified by the faquis. Conde, i. 420.

[3] Murphy, "Hist. of Moh. Empire in Spain," p. 232.

[4] Conde, i. p. 457.   [5] For others see Conde, i. 483, 484.

was forbidden by Mohammedan law,[1] the women being obliged to perform their devotions at home; "if," says Sale, "they visit the mosques, it must be when the men are not there; for the Moslems are of opinion that their presence inspires a different kind of devotion from that which is requisite in a place dedicated to the service of God." Sale also quotes from the letter of a Moor, censuring the Roman Catholic manner of performing the mass, for the reason, among others, that women were there. If the evidence of ballads be accepted, we shall find the Moorish ladies appearing at festivities and dances.[2] At tournaments they looked on, their bright smiles heartening the knights on to do brave deeds, and their fair hands giving the successful champion the meed of victorious valour.[3] Their position, in fact, as Prescott remarks, became assimilated to that of Christian ladies.

The effect of this improvement in the social position of women could not fail to reflect itself in the conception of love among the Spanish Arabs; and, accordingly, we find their gross sensuality undergoing a process of refinement, as the following extract from Said ibn Djoudi,[4] who wrote at the close of the ninth century, will shew. Addressing his ideal mistress, Djehama, he says:—

> " O thou, to whom my prayers are given,
>   Compassionate and gentle be
>   To my poor soul, so roughly driven,
>   To fly from me to thee.
>
> " I call thy name, my vows outpouring,
>   I see thine eyes with tear-drops shine :
>   No monk, his imaged saint adoring,
>   Knows rapture like to mine ! "

---

[1] Sale, Introd., Koran, p. 84. (Chandos Classics.)
[2] Prescott, "Ferd. and Isab.," p. 158.
[3] See a picture in the Alhambra, given in Murphy's "Moorish Antiquities of Spain," Lockhart, Pref., p. 13; and the ballad called "The Bullfight of Ghazal," st. v. p. 109.   [4] Killed, 897.

Of these words Dozy [1] says :—" They might be those of a Provençal troubadour. They breathe the delicateness of Christian chivalry."

This Christianising of the feeling of love is even more clearly seen in a passage from a treatise on Love by Ali ibn Hazm, who was prime minister to Abdurrahman V. (Dec. 1023-Mar. 1024). He calls Love [2] a mixture of moral affection, delicate gallantry, enthusiasm, and a calm modest beauty, full of sweet dignity. Being the great grandson of Christian parents, perhaps some of their inherited characteristics reappeared in him :—" Something pure, something delicate, something spiritual which was not Arab." [3]

———o———

CHAPTER XI.

INFLUENCE OF ISLAM ON CHRISTIANITY.

WE have so far investigated the influence of Christianity on the social and intellectual character of Mohammedanism ; let us now turn to the analogous influence of Mohammedanism on Christianity under the same aspects. This, as was to be expected, is by no means so marked as in the reverse case. One striking instance, however, there is, in which such an influence was shewn, and where we should least have thought to find it. We have indisputable evidence that many Christians submitted to be circumcised. Whether this was for the sake of passing themselves off on occasion as Mussulmans, or for some other reason, we cannot be certain: but the fact remains. [4] " Have we not," says Alvar, [5]

[1] II. 229.   [2] Quoted by Dozy, iii. 350.   [3] Dozy, l.l.
[4] See John of Cordova, in the "Life of John of Gorz," above, p. 89.
[5] Alvar, "Ind. Lum.," sec. 35.

"the mark of the beast, when setting at nought the customs of the fathers, we follow the pestilent ways of the Gentiles; when, neglecting the circumcision of the heart,[1] which is chiefly commanded us, we submit to the corporeal rite, which ought to be avoided for its ignominy, and which can only be complied with at the cost of no small pain to ourselves."

Even bishops did not shrink from conforming to this Semitic rite,[2] whether voluntarily, or under compulsion, we cannot say; but we know that the Mohammedan king, under whom this occurred, had at one time the intention of forcing all his Christian subjects to be circumcised.[3]

Another sign of an approximation made by Christians to the outward observances of Moslems, was that some among them thought it necessary to abstain from certain meats,[4] those, namely, forbidden by the Mohammedan law.

A bishop, being taxed with compliance of this kind, gave as his excuse that otherwise the Christians could not live with the Saracens.[5] This was, naturally, not considered a good reason by the stricter or more bigoted party, who regarded with alarm and suspicion any tendency towards amalgamation with Mohammedans. If we can credit certain chroniclers, a council was even held some years before this time by Basilius, Bishop of Cordova, for considering the best method of preventing the contamination of the purity of the Christian faith by its contact with Mohammedanism.[6]

---

[1] Romans ii. 29; Galatians v. 2.

[2] See "Life of John of Gorz," sec. 123.

[3] See "Life of John of Gorz," sec. 123; Samson, "Apolog.," ii. c. 4. Cp. "Loys de Mayerne Turguet," xvii. 13. The king, Halihatan (Abdurrahman III.), 950, published an edict, "par lequel il estait mandé a tous Chrestiens habitans és terres et villes a luy subjectes de laisser la religion de Jesu, et se faisans circoncire prendre cette de Mahomet, sur peine de vie."

[4] See Appendix B, p. 167; and Koran v. *ad init.*—"You are forbidden to eat that which dieth of itself, and blood, and swine's flesh . . . and that which hath been strangled."   [5] "John of Gorz," l.l.

[6] "Pseudo-Luit.," sec. 341.   Cp. "Chron. Juliani," sec. 501.

Sometimes, however, the contact with Islam acted by way of contraries, and Christian bigots, such as the monks often were, would cling to some habit or rite of their own from a mere spirit of opposition to a reverse custom among Moslems. Thus we know that the monks in the East became the more passionately devoted to their image-worship, because Iconoclasm savoured so much of Mohammedanism. In the same way, but with far more objectionable results, the clergy in Spain did their best to impress the people with the idea that cleanliness of apparel and person, far from being next to godliness, was incompatible with it, and that baths were the direct invention of the devil.[1] Later on we know that Philip II., the husband of our Queen Mary, had all public baths in his Spanish dominions destroyed, on the ground that they were relics of infidelity.[2]

Celibacy of the clergy, again, was strongly advocated as a contrast to the polygamy of Mohammedans; and an abbot, Saulus, is mentioned with horror as having a wife and children, one of whom afterwards succeeded him, and also married.[3]

One of the last acts of a Gothic king had been to enforce the marriage of the clergy, and though this act was repealed by Fruela I. (757-768) in the North, yet concubinage became very common among the clergy;[4] and it was perhaps to remedy a similar state of things that Witiza wished to compel the clergy to have lawful wives.

"Viritanus coegit concilium Toleto ad inveniendum remedium ne Muzarabes Toletani, imo totius Hispaniae, Saracenis coniuncti, illorum caeremoniis communicarent."   [1] Miss Yonge, p. 67.

[2] Lane-Poole, "Story of the Moors," p. 136.

[3] Florez, "Esp. Sagr.," xviii. 326—"Conventus Episcoporum pro restoratione monasterii." The children are called "Spinae ac vepres, nec nominandi proles."

[4] Prescott, "Ferd. and Isab.," p. 16. From Samson, "Apol.," ii. cc. 2, 6, we learn that Christians had begun to imitate the Moslems in having harems.

We have left to the last the great and interesting question of the origin of chivalry. Though forming no part of the doctrines of Christianity or Islam, chivalry and its influences could not with justice be wholly overlooked in a discussion like the present. The institution known by that name arose in the age of Charles the Great (768-814),[1] and was therefore nearly synchronous with the invasion of Europe by the Arabs. Its origin has been, indeed, referred to the military service of fiefs, but all its characteristics, which were personal and individual, such as loyalty, courtesy, munificence, point to a racial rather than a political source, and these characteristics are found in an eminent degree among the Arabs. "The solitary and independent spirit of chivalry," says Hallam,[2] "dwelling as it were upon a rock, and disdaining injustice or falsehood from a consciousness of internal dignity, without any calculation of the consequences, is not unlike what we sometimes read of Arabian chiefs or American Indians."

Whatever the precise origin of chivalry may have been, there can be no doubt that its development was largely influenced by the relative positions of Arabs and Christians in Spain, and the perpetual war which went on between them in that country.

Though not a religious institution at the outset, except perhaps among our Saxon forefathers,[3] chivalry soon became religious in character, and its golden age of splendour was during the crusades against the Moslems of Spain and Palestine. Spain itself may almost be called the cradle of chivalry; and it must be allowed that even in the first flush

---

[1] Hallam, " Mid. Ages.," iii. 392.

[2] *Ibid.* Cp. p. 402. "The characteristic virtues of chivalry have so much resemblance to those which Eastern writers of the same period extol, that I am disposed to suspect Europe for having derived some improvement from imitation of Asia."

[3] Hallam, " Mid. Ages " (l.l.).

of conquest the Arabs shewed themselves to be truly chivalrous enemies, and clearly had nothing to learn from Christians in that respect. The very earliest days of Moslem triumph saw the same chivalrous spirit displayed at the capture of Jerusalem, forming a strange and melancholy contrast to the scene at its recapture subsequently by the Crusaders under the heroic Godfrey de Bouillon.

Similarly the last triumph of the Moors in Spain, at the end of the tenth century, furnished an instance of generosity rarely paralleled. The Almohade king, Yakub Almansur, after the great victory of Alarcos (1193), released 20,000 Christian prisoners. It cannot, however, be denied that the action displeased many of the king's followers, who complained of it "as one of the extravagancies proper to monarchs,"[1] and Yakub himself repented of it on his deathbed.

In many passages of the Arabian writers we find those qualities enumerated which ought to distinguish the Moorish knight—such. as piety, courtesy, prowess in war, the gift of eloquence, the art of poetry, skill on horseback, and dexterity with sword, lance, and bow.[2] Chivalry soon became a recognised art, and we hear of a certain Yusuf ben Harun, or Abu Amar, addressing an elegant poem to Hakem II. (961-976) on its duties and obligations;[3] nor was it long before the Moorish kings learnt to confer knighthood on their vassals after the Christian fashion, and we have an instance of this in a knighthood conferred by the king of Seville in 1068.[4]

As the ideal knight of Spanish romance was Ruy Diaz de Bivar, or the Cid, so we may perhaps regard the historic Almanzor as the Moorish knight *sans peur et sans reproche;* and though, if judged by our standards, he was by no means

[1] Conde, iii. 53.
[2] Al Makk., ii. 401, from Ibn Hayyan. Cp. Prescott, "Ferd. and Isab.," p. 159.　　　　[3] Conde, i. 477.　　　　[4] Conde, ii. 173.

sans reproche, yet many are the stories told of his magnanimity and justice. On one occasion after a battle against the Christians, the Count of Garcia being mortally wounded, his faithful Castilians refused to leave him, and were hemmed in by Almanzor's men. When the latter was urged to give the word, and have the knot of Christians put to the sword, he said: "Is it not written? ' He who slayeth one man, not having met with violence, will be punished like the murderer of all mankind, and he who saveth the life of one man, shall be rewarded like the rescuer of all.' [1] Make room, sons of Ishmael, make way; let the Christians live and bless the name of the clement and merciful God." [2]

On another occasion Almanzor is asked by the Count of Lara for wedding gifts for an enemy [3] of the Arabs, another Christian count, and he magnanimously sends the gifts ; or we see him releasing the father of the Infantes of Lara, on hearing of the dreadful death of his seven sons. [4]

It must be admitted that these instances savour too much of the romantic ballad style, but anecdotes of generosity do not gather round any but persons who are noted for that virtue, and though the instances should be false in letter, yet in spirit they may be eminently true. However this may be as respects Almanzor's generosity, of his justice we have unimpeachable evidence. The monk who wrote the " Chronicle of Silo," says that the success of his raids on the Christian territories was due to the large pay he offered his soldiers, and also to his extreme justice, " which virtue," says the chronicler, " as I learned from my father's lips, Almanzor held dearer, if I may so say, than any Christian." [5]

In connection with chivalry there is one institution which the Christian Spaniards seem to have borrowed from the Moors—those military orders, namely, which were so numerous in Spain. " The Rabitos, or Moslemah knights," says

---

[1] Koran, v. 35. [2] Yonge, p. 110. [3] *Ibid.*, p. 80.
[4] Johannes Vasaeus, 969. [5] " Chron. Sil.," sec. 70.

Conde,[1] " in charge of the frontier, professed extraordinary austerity of life, and devoted themselves voluntarily to the continual exercise of arms. They were all men of high distinction ; and bound themselves by a vow to defend the frontier. They were forbidden by their rules to fly from the enemy, it being their duty to fight and die on the spot they held."

In any case, whether the Christian military orders were derived from the Moorish, or the reverse, one thing is certain, that it was the Moors who inoculated the Christians with a belief in Holy Wars, as an essential part of their religion.[2] In this respect Christianity became Mohammedanized first in Spain. Chivalry became identified with war against the infidel, and found its apotheosis[3] in St James of Compostella, who—a poor fisherman of Galilee—was supposed to have fought in person against the Moors at Clavijo.[4] In the ballad we hear of Christian knights coming to engage in fight from exactly that same belief in the efficacy and divine institution of holy wars, as animated the Arab champions. The clergy, and even the bishops, took up arms and fought against the enemies of their faith. Two bishops, those of Leon and Astorga,[5] were taken prisoners at the battle of Val de Junqueras (921).[6] Sisenandus of Compostella was killed in

---

[1] Conde, ii. p. 119, note—"It seems highly probable that from these arose the military orders of Spain in the East." Cp. Prescott, " Ferd. and Isab.," p. 122. The military orders of Spain were mostly instituted by papal bulls in the last half of the 12th century.

[2] Islam made Christianity military, Milman, "Lat. Chr.," ii. pp. 220-2. Lecky, "Hist. Eur. Moral," p. 262, ff.

[3] Presc., " Ferd.," p. 15.

[4] Mohammed also imagined celestial aid in battle, see Kor. iii., ad init.

[5] " Rodrigo of Toledo," iii. p. 4. Johannes Vasaeus says they were the bishops of Tuy and Salamanca.

[6] Mariana, viii. 5. See also *Ibid.*, c. 6.

battle against the Northmen (979) ; and the "Chronicle of the Cid" makes repeated mention of a right valiant prelate named Hieronymus.[1]

Yet, in spite of all this, in spite of the fanaticism which engendered and accompanied it, chivalry proved to be the only common ground on which Christian and Moslem, Arab and European, could meet. It was in fact a sort of compromise between two incompatible religions mutually accepted by two different races. Though perhaps not a spiritual religion, it was a social one, and served in some measure to mitigate the horrors of a war of races and creeds. Chivalry culminated in the Crusades, and Richard I. of England and Saladin were the Achilles and the Hector of a new Iliad.

With this short discussion of the origin and value of chivalry as a compromise between Christianity and Mohammedanism, we will now conclude. In discussing the relations between Christianity and Mohammedanism, we have been naturally led to compare not only the religions but their adherents, for it is difficult to distinguish between those who profess a creed, and the creed which they profess ; but at least we may have thus been enabled to avoid missing any point essential to the proper elucidation of the mutual relations which existed between the two greatest religions of the world, and the influence they had upon each other.

---

[1] "Chronicle of Cid" (Southey), p. 371.

APPENDIX.

A.

THE JEWS IN SPAIN.

THE persecution of the Jews by the Gothic Spaniards naturally made them the implacable enemies of the Christians. Being a very numerous colony in Spain—for Hadrian had transported thither many thousand families—the Jews gave the Arabs very effective help in conquering the country, both by betraying places to them, and garrisoning captured towns while the Arabs went on to fresh conquests. Consequently the relations between the Jews and Moslems were for a long time very cordial, though this cordiality wore off in the course of time. Their numbers seem to have been considerable under the Moslem occupation, and whole towns were set apart as Jewries.[1]

In France the prejudice against the Jews shewed itself very strongly among the clergy, though Louis I. and his wife Judith favoured them. They were generally ill-treated, and their slaves were induced by the clergy to be baptized. Thereupon they became free, as Jews were not allowed to have Christian slaves.[2] But it must be admitted that the Franks had reason for disliking the Jews, as it was well known that they sold Christian children as slaves to the Moslems of Spain.[3]

They also seem to have been able to make some proselytes from among the Christians, and we hear of one apos-

---

[1] Al Makkari, ii. 452. [2] Fleury, v. 408. [3] *Ibid.*

tate of this kind, named Eleazar, to whom Alvar addressed
several letters under the title of "the transgressor." This
man's original name was Bodon. A Christian of German
extraction,[1] he was brought up with a view to Holy Orders.
In 838, while on his way to Rome,[2] he apostatised to
Judaism,[3] and opened a negotiation with the Jews in France
to sell his companions as slaves, stipulating only to keep
his own grandson. The next year he let his hair and beard
grow, and went to Spain, where he married a Jewess, com-
pelling his grandson at the same time to apostatise. In
845 or 847 his attitude became so hostile to the Christians
in Spain, that the latter wrote to Charles, praying him to
demand Eleazar as his subject, which however does not
seem to have been done. There seems good reason to
believe that Eleazar stirred up the Moslems against the
Christians, and the deaths of Prefectus and John may have
been due to him.[4] After this we hear no more of Eleazar;
but the position of the Jews with regard to the Arabs seems
to have been for long after this of a most privileged character. Consequently the Jews in Spain had such an opportunity to develop their natural gifts as they have never had
since the capture of Jerusalem by Nebuchadnezzar; and
they shewed themselves no whit behind the Arabs, if indeed they did not outstrip them, in keeping alive the flame
of learning in the dark ages.[5] In science generally, and
especially in the art of medicine they had few rivals, and in
learning and civilisation they were, no less than the Arabs,
far ahead of the Christians.[6]

The good understanding between the Jews and the Arabs

---

[1] "Ann. Bertin.," 839.   [2] Orationis gratia, "Ann. Bert.," l.l.
[3] Florez, xi. p. 20 ff.
[4] The "Ann. Bert." say that he induced Abdurrahman II. to give his
Christian subjects the choice between Islam, Judaism, or death. See
Rohrbacher, xii. 4.
[5] Prescott, "Ferd. and Isab." p. 153.   [6] *Ibid.*, p. 134.

with the gradual process of time gave place to an ill-concealed hostility, and at the beginning of the twelfth century there seems even to have been a project formed for forcing the Jews to become Moslems on the ground of a promise made by their forefathers to Mohammed that, if in five centuries their Messiah had not appeared, they would be converted to Mohammedanism.[1]   Perhaps this was only a pretext on the part of the Moslems for extorting money; at all events the Jews only succeeded in evading the alternative by paying a large sum of money.   Even in the early years of the conquest they were subject to the rapacity of their rulers, for when, on the rumour of the Messiah having appeared in Syria, many of the Spanish Jews, leaving their goods, started off to join him, the Moslem governor, Anbasa, seized the property so left, and refused to restore it on the return of the disappointed emigrants.

From their contact with Arabs and Christians the Jews seem to have lost many of their distinctive beliefs, and in the twelfth century Maimonides,[2] the greatest name among the Spanish Jews, wrote against their errors.   One of these seems to have been that the books of Moses were written before the Creation;[3] another, that there was a series of hells in the next world.[4]

Many Jews attained to very high positions among the Arabs, and we hear of a certain Hasdai ibn Bahrut, who was inspector of customs to Abdurrahman III., ambassador to the King of Leon in 955, and the king's confidential messenger to the monk, John of Gorz, a few years later. He was also distinguished as a physician.[5]

While the Arabs still retained their hold on the fairest provinces of Spain, the lot of the Jews, even in Christian

---

[1] Conde, ii. 326.   [2] Fleury, v. 409.
[3] Cp. the Moslem belief about the Koran.   Sale, Introduc., p. 50. (Chandos Classics.)   [4] *Ibid.*, p. 72.
[5] Al Makk., i., App. v. p. xxiv.   Note by De Gayangos.

territories, was by no means unendurable. They were sometimes advanced to important and confidential posts, and it
was the murder of Alfonso VI.'s Jewish ambassador by the
King of Seville which brought about the introduction of the
Almoravides into Spain.

There is a strange story told of the Jews at the taking of
Toledo by the Christians in 1085. They waited on Alfonso
and assured him that they were part of the ten tribes whom
Nebuchadnezzar transported into Spain, and not the descendants of those Jerusalem Jews who crucified Christ.
Their ancestors, they said, were quite free from the guilt of
this act, for when Caiaphas had written to the Toledan syna-
gogue for their advice respecting the person who claimed to
be the Messiah, the Toledan Jews returned for answer, that
in their judgment the prophecies seemed to be fulfilled in
Him, and therefore He ought not by any means to be
put to death. This reply they produced in the original
Hebrew.[1] It is needless to say that the whole thing was a
fabrication.

Gradually, as the Christians recovered their supremacy in
Spain, the tide of prejudice set more and more strongly
against the Jews. They were accused of "contempt for the
Catholic worship, desecration of its symbols, sacrifice of
Christian infants,"[2] and other enormities. Severe laws were
passed against them, as in the old Gothic times, and their
freedom was grievously curtailed in the matters of dress,
residence, and profession. As a distinctive badge they had
to wear yellow caps.[3]

At the end of the fourteenth century the people rose
against them, and 15,000 Jews were massacred in different
parts of Spain. Many were nominally converted, and 35,000
conversions were put to the credit of a single saint. These

[1] Southey, "Roder.," i. p. 235, note.
[2] Prescott, "Ferd. and Isab.," pp. 134, 135.
[3] Al Makk., i. 116.

new Christians sometimes attained high ecclesiastical digni-
ties, and intermarried with the noble families—the taint of
which "mala sangre" came afterwards to be regarded with
the greatest horror and aversion.

It was against the converted Jews that the Inquisition
was first established, and they chiefly suffered under it
at first. In 1492, on the final extinction of the Arab
dominion in Spain, a very large number of Jews were expelled from Castile,[1] the evil example being afterwards followed in other parts of Spain. The story of the treatment
of Jews by Christians is indeed one of the darkest in the
history of Christianity.

B.

SPAIN AND THE PAPAL POWER.

Perhaps no part of the history of Spain affords so in
teresting a study as the consideration of those gradual
steps by which, from being one of the most independent
of Churches, she has become the most subservient, and
therefore the most degraded, of all. The question of how
this was brought about, apart from its intrinsic interest as
illustrating the development of a great nation, is well worth
investigating, from the momentous influence which it has
had upon the religious history of the world at large. For it
is not too much to say that Rome could never have made
good its ascendency, spiritual no less than temporal, over
so large a part of mankind, had not the material resources
and the blind devotion of Spain been ready to back the
haughty pretensions and unscrupulous ability of the Italian
pontiffs.

In fact, Spain is the only country, apart from Italy, that
as a nation, has accepted the monstrous doctrines of Rome

---

[1] Variously estimated at 160,000 or 800,000.

in all their entirety—doctrines which the whole Christian East repudiated from the first with scorn, and which the North and (with the exception of Spain) the West of Europe —the birthplace and cradle of the mighty Teutonic races —have agreed with equal disdain to reject and trample under their feet.

This result is all the more remarkable, from the fact that in early times the Church of Spain, from its rapid extension, its greatness, and its prosperity, held a position of complete equality with the Roman and other principal churches. The See of Cordova held so high a rank in the fourth century that Hosius, its venerable bishop, was chosen to preside at the important councils of Nice (325) and Sardica (347).

The Gothic invasion at the beginning of the fifth century made Spain still less likely to acknowledge any supremacy of Rome, for the Goths, besides being far more independent in character than the Romanized Kelts, were Arian heretics, and cut off, in consequence, from all communion with Rome. The orthodox party, however, gradually gained strength, and in 560 the remnants of the Suevi abjured Arianism, and the Gothic king's son Ermenegild, with their help, revolted against his father. He was finally put to death for his treason, but his brother, Recared, on ascending the throne in 589, avowed his conversion to the orthodox creed, his example being followed by most of his nobles and prelates.

The reception of Recared and his Court into the Catholic fold was the signal for an attempt to establish the papal authority, which was the more dangerous now, as the popes had gained a great increase of power since Spain was cut off from orthodox Christendom by the invasion of the Arian Goths.

One of Recared's first acts was to write to the pope and, saluting him, ask him for his advice in spiritual matters.

The papal authority thus acknowledged was soon exercised in—

(*a.*) Deciding ecclesiastical appeals without regard to the laws of the land;

(*b.*) Sending to Spain pontifical judges to hear such cases;

(*c.*) Sending legates to watch over the discipline of the Church;

(*d.*) Sending the pall to metropolitans.

These metropolitans, unknown in the earlier history of the Spanish Church, came gradually to be recognised, owing to the papal practice of sending letters to the chief bishops of the country. They became invested in consequence with certain important powers, such as those of convoking provincial councils; of consecrating suffragans; of holding ecclesiastical courts, and watching over the conduct of bishops.[1]

But though a certain authority over the Spanish Church *was* thus conceded to the pope, yet owing to the independent spirit of the Spanish kings and clergy, he contented himself with a very sparing use of his power. In two points, in especial, the claims of the pope were strenuously resisted.

(*a.*) The purchase of dispensations from Rome was expressly forbidden.

(*b.*) Papal infallibility was a dogma by no means admitted. Thus the prelates of Spain in the fifteenth and sixteenth councils of Toledo, defended the orthodoxy of their fellow-bishop, Julian, against the strictures of the then pope, Bendict II.; and Benedict's successor, John V., confessed that they had been in the right.[2]

This spirit of opposition to the supremacy of the pope we find manifested to the last by the Spanish kings, and there is some reason for thinking that in the very year of the Saracen invasion the king, Witiza, held a synod, which

[1] Masdeu, xi. p. 167, ff., quoted by Dr Dunham.
[2] Dunham, i. p. 197.

emphatically forbade appeals to Rome.[1]   One author even goes so far as to say that the Gothic king and his clergy being at variance with the pope, the latter encouraged and favoured the Saracen invasion.[2]

However that may have been, and it certainly looks very improbable, the invasion did not help the pope much directly, though indirectly, and as events turned out, the Arab domination was undoubtedly the main cause of the ultimate subjection of Spain to the papal yoke, which happened in this way:—The Christian Church in the North being, though free, yet in a position of great danger and weakness, would naturally have sought help from their nearest Christian neighbours, the Franks.   But the selfish and ambitious policy of the latter, who preferred extending their temporal dominion to fighting as champions of Christianity in defence of others, naturally forced the Spanish Christians to look to the only Christian ruler who could afford them even moral assistance; and the popes were not slow to avail themselves of the opportunity thus offered for establishing their authority in a new province.   It was by the intervention of the popes that the war against the Arabs partook of the nature of a crusade, a form of warfare which carried with it the advantage of filling the treasury of the Bishops of Rome.   By means of indulgences, granting exemption from purgatory at 200 maravedis a head, the pope collected in four years the sum of four million maravedis.[3]

The first important instance of the Pope's intervention being asked and obtained was in 808, when, the body of St James being miraculously discovered, Alfonso wrote to the pope asking leave to move the see of Ira Flavia (Padron) to the new church of St Iago,[4] built on the spot where the relics

---

[1] See Hardwicke's "Church in the Middle Ages," p. 42.   He quotes Gieselar, "Ch. Hist.," iii. 132.

[2] J. S. Semler, quoted by Mosheim, ii. 120, note.

[3] Prescott, "Ferd. and Isab.," p. 64, n.

[4] Romey, "Hist. d'Esp.," iii. 420.

were found. The birth of the new Spanish Church dates from this event, which was of ominous import for the future independence of the Church in that country. What the claims of Rome had come to be within a quarter of a century of this epoch, we may see from the controversy which arose between Claudius, Bishop of Turin, and the papal party. Claudius was himself a Spaniard, and a pupil of the celebrated Felix, Bishop of Urgel, one of the authors of the Adoptionist heresy. Among other doctrines obnoxious to the so-called Catholic party, Claudius stoutly resisted the papal claim to be the head of Christendom, resting his opposition, so far as we can gather from what remains to us of his writings,[1] on the grounds, first, that Christ did *not* say to Peter, "What thou loosest in heaven, shall be loosed upon earth;" meaning by this that the authority vested in Peter was only to be exercised during his life; secondly, in answer to the supposed efficacy of a pilgrimage to Rome, Claudius retorts on his accuser, Theodomir, abbot of a monastery near Nîmes:—"If a doing of penance to be effectual involves a journey to Rome, why do you keep so many monks in your monastery and prevent them from going—as you say is necessary—to Rome itself?" As to the journey itself, Claudius said that he neither approved nor disapproved of it, knowing that it was not prejudicial to all, nor useful to all: but this he was assured of, that eternal life could not be gained by a mere journey to Rome; thirdly, as to the pope being the Dominicus Apostolicus, as his supporters called him, apostolic, says Claudius, is a title that does not belong to one "who fills the see of an apostle, but who fulfils the duties thereof."

Being summoned to appear before a council, the bishop proved contumacious, and refused to go, calling the proposed assemblage a congregation of asses. In spite of his

[1] Jonas of Orleans, iii., apud Migne, vol. civ. p. 375 ff. Fleury, v. 398.

independence of spirit Claudius remained Bishop of Turin till his death in 839.

The pope's authority being once recognised in Spain, the sphere of his interference rapidly enlarged, and we soon find the king unable even to call a council of bishops without a papal bull.   This became the established practice.[1]   In the tenth century Bermudo II. (982-999), in confirming the laws of the Goths, took the opportunity to make the canons and decrees of the pope binding in secular cases.[2]

Meanwhile, even before the free Christians in the North had established their independence, the weakness of the Christian Church under Arab domination seemed to afford a good opportunity for obtaining from them a recognition of the authority of the pope.   We accordingly find that an appeal was made to the pope towards the close of the eighth century to give an authoritative decision with regard to what the appellants deemed to be certain irregularities which had found their way into the practice of those Christians who were under the Arab yoke.   The Pope Adrian readily undertook to define what was, and what was not, in accordance with Christianity.   In a letter addressed to the Bishops of Spain he inveighs against the following errors, countenanced by a certain Migetius, and by Egila, Bishop of Elvira, and sometimes called in consequence the Migetian errors :—

(*a.*) The wrong celebration of Easter.   This had already been noticed and condemned by Peter, a deacon of Toledo, in a letter to the people of Seville (750).[3]   The error was not the same as that of the Quarto-decimani, but consisted

---

[1] "Chron. Sil.," sec. 13, who says that in 1109 a legate was in Spain holding a council at Leon.   "Chron. Sampiri," (Florez, xiv.), sec. 6 (a later addition), says that in 869 Alfonso IV. sent Severus and Sideric, asking the leave of Pope John VIII. to hold a council and consecrate a church.   Cp. Mariana, vii. 8.   [2] Mariana, viii. 6.

[3] Isid. Pac., sec. 77.   See Migne, vol. xcviii. pp. 339, 376, 451.

apparently in deferring Easter to the twenty-second day, if the full moon fell on the 14th, and the following day was Sunday. Curiously enough this very error had been held by the Latin Church itself till the sixth century.[1] The fulminations of the Pope failed in suppressing the error. As late as 891 it was sufficiently general in Andalusia to cause the date of a battle which took place at the Easter of that year to be placed in the year of the Hegira 278, which only began on April 15th, whereas had Easter been observed according to the usage of the Latin Church, the Paschal feast would have been already past.[2]

(*b.*) The eating of pork and things strangled.[3] With respect to these innocent articles of food, the pope goes so far as to threaten anathema against those who will not abstain from them. It is curious to find the Christian Church upholding the eating of pork, when brought into contact with the Moslems, and forbidding it elsewhere.

(*c.*) Intermarriage with Jews and Moslems, which had become very common, is denounced and forbidden.[4]

(*d.*) The Pope cautions the Spanish Church against consecrating priests without due preparation, and speaks as if there were many false priests, wolves in sheep's clothing, dealing havoc in the flock.

(*e.*) One doubtful authority,[5] who tells us that Adrian ordered Cixila, Bishop of Toledo, to hold a council and condemn Egila for not fasting on Sundays, according to the decrees of previous popes.

---

[1] See Victorius Aquitanus, quoted by Noris "de Paschali Latinorum Cyclo." (iii. 786), apud Migne.

[2] Dozy, ii. p. 355, note.

[3] Florez, "Esp. Sagr.," v. 514 : Fleury, ii. 235.

[4] Adrian's Letter to the Spanish Bishops.

[5] The Pseudo-Luitprand, sec. 236—" Ex mandatis litterisque Adriani papae contra Egilanum . . . nolentem Dei Sabbate a carnibus abstinere" (776 A.D.).

But though there was a strong party in Spain favouring
the pretensions of the pope, yet many of the clergy and
laity, headed by the venerable Elipandus, Bishop of Toledo
(782-810), boldly resisted the encroachments of the Bishop
of Rome. Elipandus himself, as Primate of all Spain, wrote
to Migetius condemning him for certain heresies, and boasts
of having completely refuted and silenced him;[1] but at
the same time Elipandus shewed his independence of the
Roman Pontiff by characterising those who abstained from
pork and things strangled as foolish and ignorant men ;
though Migetius in this matter was in thorough accord with
the pope,[2] and could justify his views by a reference to the
decision of the Church of Jerusalem in the earliest days of
Christianity.[3]

Another doctrine combated by Elipandus was the un-
scriptural one, that it was unlawful to eat with unbelievers,
or even to take food touched by them. It was easy for him
to quote texts such as : " Not that which entereth into the
mouth defileth the man ; but that which proceedeth out of
the mouth, this defileth the man;"[4] or "to the pure all things
are pure;"[5] and to point out that Christ ate with publicans
and sinners.

But the assumption which Elipandus, like his fellow-
countrymen, Claudius of Turin, later, especially attacked,
was that which regarded the Roman See as alone constituting the Catholic Church and the power of God.[6] This he
very properly calls a heresy ; and indignantly denies that

---

[1] Epilandus, Letter to Migetius.   Migne, xcviii. p. 859.   See
Neander, v. 216 ff. n.   Enhueber, "Dissert.," secs. 29, 33, apud
Migne, vol. ci.   [2] See Adrian's Letter to Egila.

[3] Acts xv. 19, 29. See, however, Epist. to Timothy, i. 3.

[4] St Matt. xv. 11.   [5] Titus i. 15.

[6] See also letter to Alcuin, and Felix's answer to Alcuin's first book,
where he gives us his idea of a *Catholic* church founded on our Lord
Christ (and not on the pope), . . . which Catholic church may even
consist of few members. Neander, v. 230.

Christ's words, "Thou art Peter," &c., apply to the Church
of Rome alone, affirming that they were spoken of the
whole Church. "How," he adds, "can the Roman Church
be, as you say it is, the very power of God without spot
or blemish, when we know that at least one bishop of
Rome (Liberius) has been branded as a heretic by the
common voice of Christendom."

Had the Arab domination embraced the whole of Spain,
and continued to be established over it, Spain could never
have become the priest-ridden country which it now is;
but the gradual advance of the Christian arms in the North
brought in its train a more and more complete subserviency
to the pope.

As the kings of Castile and Leon gradually won back
towns and provinces from the Arabs, some difference was
observed to exist between the religious usages of the newly
freed Christians and of those who had set them free. This
was specially apparent in the old Gothic liturgy, which the
Muzarabic Christians had used all along, and were still
using, whereas the Christians of Leon and the Asturias had
imported a newer recension from Rome.

Rumours of these discrepancies in religious ritual reached
Rome, and accordingly a legate,[1] named Zanclus, was sent
to Spain in 925 from John X. to inquire into matters of
religion, and particularly into the ceremony of the mass,
the opinion being prevalent at Rome that the mass was
incorrectly performed according to the Gothic liturgy, and
that false doctrines were taught. However, Zanclus found
that the divergence was not sufficiently wide to warrant the
suppression of the ancient ritual. It may be that the power
of the Roman Church was not established so securely as
to admit of an interference so unpalatable to the ancient
church. She was content to bide her time; for such a

---

[1] Mariana, vi. 9. Pseudo-Luit. gives the legate the name of Marinus,
and says he was sent in 932 to Basilius, Bishop of Toledo.

standing witness to the primitive usage [1] of the Church against the innovations of the Roman See could not long be allowed to continue.   Accordingly, we find that very soon after the fall of Toledo in 1085, the question of the old Gothic liturgy came up for discussion again.   The Gothic and the Roman books were subjected, after the absurd fashion of the times, to two ordeals—by water and by fire; but in spite of the fact that the Gothic liturgy, thanks to its greater solidity and stronger binding, resisted both those elements incomparably better than its younger rival, and so, if the ordeal went for anything, should have been hailed victorious, the old native liturgy was partially suppressed at the bidding of the pope, and by the consent of the Spanish king Alfonso VI. of Leon, [2] and Sancho IV. of Aragon.   Yet the Muzarabic Christians were loath to give up their customary liturgy, and it remained in use in several churches of Toledo till late in the fifteenth century.

But the interference of the pope was not confined to matters relating to the Spanish Church at large, his heavy hand fell upon the king himself, and at the end of the twelfth century Alfonso IX. and all his kingdom were laid under an interdict by Celestine III. because he had married within forbidden limits, and refused to divorce his wife at the bidding of the pope.   He did in the end divorce her, but only to repeat the same offence with a second wife, Berengaria, and incur the same penalty at the hands of Innocent III.   Encroachments on the king's power went on apace, and gradually appeals came to be referred to Rome from the king's courts, and the pope took upon himself to appoint to benefices and bishoprics; a usurpation which

---

[1] Cp. the monstrous way in which the Portuguese Roman Catholics, under Don Alexis de Menezes, destroyed the sacred books and memorials of the ancient Syrian Church on the Malabar coast in India.

[2] And I. of Castile.

was countenanced by Alfonso X. (1252-1284).[1] But this result was not attained without remonstrances from the Cortes, and finally, under Ferdinand and Isabella, the question came to an open rupture between the Spanish Court and the reigning pope, Sixtus IV. Isabella, though so ready to submit herself in matters of personal religion to the pope and his legates, refused, like her later namesake of England, to bate one jot of her ecclesiastical rights; and the pope had to give way, contenting himself with the barren power of appointing those nominated by the sovereigns of the land. But if the sovereign was jealous of his rights, no less so were the barons of theirs, and when in the war of the barons with Henry IV. (1454-1474), the papal legate threw his influence on to the king's side, and excommunicated the rebellious barons, they firmly answered that "those who had advised the pope that he had a right to interfere in the temporal concerns of Castile had deceived him ; and that they, the barons of the kingdom, had a perfect right to depose their sovereign on sufficient grounds, and meant to exercise it."[2]

A similarly independent spirit shewed itself in Aragon. In 1213 Pedro II. died fighting against the papal persecutor of the Albigensians, and down to the time of Charles V., the princes of Aragon were at open enmity with the Roman See,[3] and the Aragonése strenuously resisted the establishment of the Inquisition.[4]

That fatal instrument of religious bigotry, the cause of more unmerited suffering and more unmixed evil than any other devised by man, whereby more innocent people passed

---

[1] Prescott, " Ferd. and Isab.," p. 15.

[2] Prescott, p. 72. Cp. the charter of Aragon, whereby the king, if he violated the charter of the realm, might be deposed, and any other *Pagan* or Christian substituted. *Ibid,* p. 23.

[3] Lockhart, Introduction to Spanish ballads, p. 9. (Chandos Classics.)

[4] Prescott, " Ferd. and Isab.," p. 26, n.

through the fire than were perhaps ever sacrificed at the altar
of Moloch, was first put into action in September 1480,
during the reign of the pious and noble-minded Isabella.[1]
The festival of Epiphany in the following year was selected
as an appropriate date for the manifestation of the first auto
da fé, when six Jews were burnt at Seville; for it was against
that unfortunate people that this inhuman persecution was
devised, or at least first used. That one year witnessed the
martyrdom of 2000 persons, and the infliction on 17,000
others of punishments only less than death itself. During
the administration of Thomas of Torquemada, which lasted
eighteen years, more than 10,000 persons perished at the
stake, nearly 100,000 were, as the phrase went, reconciled.[2]
The confiscation of property which accompanied all this
burning and imprisoning brought in enormous sums into
the coffers of the Inquisitors.

The Jews being burnt, converted, or expelled the country,
the Inquisition was turned upon the wretched Moriscoes,
as the Moors under Christian government were called, who
were oppressed and persecuted in the same way as the Jews,
and finally driven from Spain.

But a more important conquest than these—more important, that is, to the supremacy of the Roman See—was the
undoubted conquest achieved by the Inquisition over the
reforming doctrines which in the sixteenth century began
to find their way into Spain from Germany and England.
Finding a congenial soil, the reformation began to spread
in Spain with wonderful rapidity. The divines sent by
Charles V. into England were themselves converted, and
returned full of zeal for the Protestant faith—"Their success," says Geddes,[3] "was such that had not a speedy and
full stop been put to their pious labours by the merciless

---

[1] The inquisitional code was drawn up in 1233, and introduced into
Spain, 1242. Prescott.   [2] Prescott, " Ferd. and Isab.," p. 146.
[3] Miscell. Tracts.   Pref. to " Spanish Martyrs," pp. 1, ff.

Inquisition, the whole kingdom of Spain had in all likelihood been converted to the Protestant religion, in less time than any other country had ever been before." [1] So untrue is it to say that persecution always fails of its object! In Spain it has riveted the fetters, which the weakness and superstition of the earlier kings of Leon and Castile, together with the piety and misdirected enthusiasm of Isabella, placed upon a proud and once peculiarly independent people. Plunged in the depths of ignorance and imbecility, social, religious, and political, Spain affords a melancholy but instructive spectacle to the nations.

[1] Geddes, Pref. to "Spanish Martyrs," p. 3, 4, quotes a Romanist author, who says: "the number of converts was so great that had the stop which was put to that evil been delayed but two or three months longer, I am persuaded that all Spain had been put into a flame by them."

LIST OF AUTHORITIES CONSULTED.

I. ORIGINAL AUTHORITIES :—

A. Arab (in translations) :

(1.) *Ibn abd el Hakem.* "History of the Conquest of Spain," with notes by J. H. Jones, Ph.D., 1858. This work only goes down to 743.

(2.) *J. A. Conde.* "History of the Domination of the Arabs in Spain," translated from the Spanish by Mrs Foster. 3 vols. Bohn, 1854. The author (Preface, p. 2) says that "he has compiled his work from Arabian memorials and writings in such sort that those documents may be read as they were written ;" (p. 18), "The student of history may read this book as written by an Arabic author."

Older writers used to speak very highly of this work, but their modern successors cannot find a good word for it.[1] De Gayangos, the learned translator of the Arabic history of Al Makkari, though not blind to the "unmethodical arrangement of the whole work, the absence of notes and citations of authorities, and the numerous errors and contradictions,"[2] yet does not hesitate to call Conde's book the foundation of all our knowledge of the history of Mohammedan Spain. It certainly is astonishing that Conde, who points out [3] the errors of his predecessors, makes precisely the same kind of mistakes himself, not only once, but constantly. Claiming to be above all things faithful to his authorities, he is found, where those authorities can be identified, not to be faithful.

(3.) *J. C. Murphy.* "History of the Mahometan Empire in

---

[1] Stanley Lane-Poole, Preface to " Moors in Spain" (1887). Dozy, Preface to "Mussulmans in Spain," p. 6: "Conde . . . qui manquait absolumment de sens historique."

[2] As to these he might plead Al Makkari's excuse, that in transcribing or extracting the accounts of different historians some facts are sure to be repeated, and others entirely contradicted. See Al Makk., i. p. 29.   [3] Pref., p. 13 ff.

Spain," with additions by Professor Shakespear, 1816. This work is based on Mohammedan sources, those, namely, which are mostly to be found in Al Makkari's compilation. The concluding chapters on the influence, scientific and literary, exercised by the Arabs in Europe, are exhaustive and interesting.

(4.) *Ahmed ibn Mohammed Al Makkari.* "History of the Mohammedan Dynasties in Spain," being an extract from a larger work by that author, translated by Pascual de Gayangos. 2 vols. London, 1840. This work, which Dozy finds fault with for certain inaccuracies, is on the whole very trustworthy, and its notes form a perfect mine of information for the student wandering helplessly among the mazes of Arab history. Al Makkari, a native of Africa, flourished at the beginning of the seventeenth century; but he quotes from many old Arabic writers, whose evidence is most valuable. Among these are—

(a.) *Abu Bekr Mohammed ibn Omar, Ibn al Kuttiyah,* descended from the grand-daughter of Witiza; died, 877.

(β.) *Ahmed ibn Mohammed ibn Musa Arrazi,* flourished in the reign of Abdurrahman III.

(γ.) *Ibn Ghalib Temam ibn Ghalib,* of Cordova; died, 1044.

(δ.) *Abu Mohammed Ali ibn Ahmed ibn Said ibn Hazm,* born at Cordova, 994; died, 1064.

(ε). *Abu Merwan Hayyan ibn Khalf ibn Huseyn ibn Hayyan,* born at Cordova, 1006.

(ζ.) *Abul Kasim Khalf ibn Abdilmalik ibn Mesud ibn Musa Al Anssari,* Cordova, 1101-1183.

(η.) *Abul hasan Ali ibn Musa ibn Mohammed ibn Abdalmalik ibn Said* of Granada, 1214-1286.

(θ.) *Abu Zeyd Abdurrahman ibn Mohammed ibn Khaldun Ishbili,* born at Tunis, 1332; died, 1406.

B. Christian (in Latin). These are to be found in—

(1.) *Schott's* "Hispania Illustrata," 3 vols. Frankfort, 1603.

(2.) *Florez,* "España Sagrada," 26 vols., containing a most useful collection of Spanish writers, together with much information about them, written in Spanish.

(3.) *Migne's* "Patrologia," Latin and Greek, a most invaluable collection in several score volumes. The following is a list of those consulted:—

(α.) *Isidore of Beja,* "Epitome Imperatorum vel Arabum Ephemerides atque Hispaniae Chronographia," being a continuation of the Chronicle of Isidore of Seville. Migne, xcvi. pp. 1246-1280.

(β.) Chronicon *Sebastiani,* "Salmanticensis Episcopi," 672-866. (Conde, Pref., p. 7, says 672-886.) *Ibid.,* cxxix. pp. 1111-1124.

(γ.) Chronicon *Albeldense,* 866-976. (Conde, *ibid.,* says to 973.) This is also called Chronicon Emilianense. It was perhaps begun by Dulcidius, Bishop of Salamanca, and carried on by the monk Vigila. *Ibid.,* 1146.

(δ.) Chronicon *Sampiri* "Asturicensis Episcopi" (written about 1000), 869-982. Florez, "Esp. Sagr.," xiv. 438-457.

(ε.) *Chronicon regum Legionensium,* 982-1109, by Pelagius, Bishop of Oviedo—a very doubtful authority, and branded with the epithet "fabulosus." *Ibid.,* pp. 466-475.

(ζ.) Chronicon *Silensis* Monachi, written *circa* 1100. *Ibid.,* xvii. 270-330.

(η.) *Lucas of Tuy,* "Chronicon Mundi," written *circa* 1236. Schott, iv. 1-116.

(θ.) *Alfonso,* Bishop of Burgos, "Anacephalaiosis rerum Hispanarum," etc. *Ibid.,* i. 246-291.

(ι.) *Luitprand,* died 972. The Chronicon and Adversaria attributed to him are by a later hand, and extend over the years 606-960. The author of these is generally called the Pseudo-Luitprand, and very little credit can be placed in his statements. Migne, cxxxvi. pp. 770-1179.

(κ.) *Rodrigo,* Archbishop of Toledo, "History of the Arabs from Christian and Arabic Sources, carried down to 1140." He died in 1245. The work is full of irrelevant references to Scripture and to profane history. He does not even mention the Christian martyrdoms in the ninth century. Schott, "Hisp Illustr.," i. pp. 121-246

(λ.) *Annales Bertiniani,* from the French point of view. Florez, x. 570-579.

(μ.) *Johannes Vasaeus,* "Hispaniae Chronicon." Schott, i. 700 ff.

The above writers must not be regarded as of equal value. Some are valuable, but all are meagre to the last degree ; others are nearly worthless.

Other authorities there are of a different kind—not historians, but writers on incidental subjects, whose works throw great light on the history of the time. Among these are—

(a.) *Elipandus,* Bishop of Toledo ; died 810. Letters— Migne, xcvi.
    to Migetius. pp. 859-867.
    to Charles the Great. „ 867-869.
    to Albinus (Alcuin). „ 870-882.
    to Fidelis, an abbot (783). „ 918, 919.

Migne, xcvi.
    pp. 882-888.
    „   894-1030.
Ibid., ci. 1321-
1331.
Ibid., c. and ci.

(*b.*) *Felix*, Bishop of Urgel ; died 816.   Confessio fidei (799).
(*c.*) *Beatus*, Priest of Libana (or Astorga).   Letter to Elipandus.
(*d.*) *Letters of Spanish Bishops* to Bishops of Gaul.
(*e.*) *Alcuin.*   Letters—
    Ad Felicem haereticum (793).
    Ad Elipandum.
    Ad Carolum Magnum (800), sending his work against Felix.
    Epistle XC. (800),
    Epistle CXIII. (800).
    Ad Aquilam Pontificem (800).
Books—
    Adversus Felicis haeresin ad abbates et monachos.
    Gothiae missus (libellus), vii. books.
    Adversus Elipandum, iv. books.
    Epistola ad Leidradum et Nefridium Episcopum.
    Altera ad eosdem.

Ibid., xcviii. p.
373.

Ibid., p. 336.

(*f.*) *Adrian*, Pope.
    Epistola Episcopis per universam Spaniam commorantibus directa, maxime tamen Elipando, vel Ascarico (785).
    Ad Egilam Episcopum (in Spania) seu Johannem presbyterum (782).
    Ad Carolum Magnum.   Epistle lxiv.

Florez, xiii.
416.

(*g.*) Letter from *Louis the Débonnaire* to the Christians of Merida (826).

Migne, cxv.
703-966.

(*h.*) *Eulogius*, priest of Cordova, and bishop-designate of Toledo.   Died 859.
    Letter to Alvar, sending his book.
    "Documentum Martyrii," dedicated to Flora and Maria, Virgins and Martyrs, Oct. 851.
    Letter to Alvar : another letter to the same, sending "Memorialis Sanctorum Liber," 3 books.
    "Liber Apologeticus Martyrum" (857).
    "De Vita et Passione SS. Virginum Florae et Mariae."

Florez, "Esp.
Sagr.," xi.

(*i.*) *Alvar*, Paulus,[1] of Cordova, and, according to his letters, both of Jewish birth and Gothic lineage.   Died, 869, according to the Pseudo-Luitprand.

pp. 62-81.
„   81-88.
„   88-91.
„   101-129.
„   129-141.

Confessio.
Letter to John of Seville.
To the Same.
To John of Seville.
To the Same.

[1] Robertson says Peter.

---

[1] Ascribed by Luitprand, sec. 309, to Bonitus, Bishop of Toledo. Morales doubts Alvar's authorship, from there being no mention of Eulogius; but see sec. 19, where a *praesul* is spoken of.

Florez, xiv. 392.

(*w.*) *Passio St Nicholai Alsamae* regis filii et sociorum martyrum qui passi sunt apud Ledesmam.   A purely fabulous account.

Florez.

(*x.*) *Vita et passio B. Virginis Argenteae* et comitum eius qui passi sunt Cordobae, Id. Maii.

Migne, xcvi. 890-894.

(*y.*) *Life of Beatus*, by an anonymous author.   Not very trustworthy, —*e.g.*, death of Elipandus placed in 798 (sec. 8): mythical council mentioned (sec. 7).

And the following *Charters*, etc. :—

Florez, xviii. 244.

Of Alfonso III. to the Church of Auria, 826.

Ibid., xviii. 312.

Of the same to the Church of Mindumnetum, 867.

Ibid., xvii. 397.

Of Bermudo II. (982-999) to the Church of Compostella.

Ibid., xviii. 326.

Assembly of Bishops pro restauratione monasterii St Mariae de Logio a parentibus Rudesindi instaurati, 927.

II. SECONDARY AUTHORITIES:—

Schott.

(1.) "Histoire generale d'Espagne par *Loys de Mayerne Turguet.* Book xvi. (1608.)

(2.) *John de Mariana.*[1] "History of Spain." Books vi.-xi., translated from the Spanish by John Stevens. (1699.)

(3.) *Fleury*, "History of the Church," translated from the French. (1727.) Vol. v. Books xli. ff.

Migne, cxv. p. 917.

(4.) *Morales.* "Remarks on the State of the Christian Religion under the Arabs at Cordova."

Ibid., ci. 305-335.

(5.) *Froben.* "Dissertatio Historica de haeresi Elipandi et Felicis."

Ibid, ci. 338-43?.

(6.) *Enhueber's* "Dissertation against Walchius' view of Adoptionism."

(7.) *Dunham.* "History of Spain and Portugal" (Lardner), 1832.   Buckle, "Civilization in England," p. 430, says of this history, very extravagantly, that it is "perhaps the best history in the English language of a foreign modern country."   It certainly has the merit—no small one in so confused a period—of being clear and succinct ; but he has a bias against the Moors.

(8.) *W. H. Prescott.* "Ferdinand and Isabella."   An excellent work.   The parts chiefly bearing on the present subject are the Introduction and chapter viii.   The great drawback to the work is the want of direct citations of authorities used.

(9.) *Hardwicke's* "History of the Christian Church in the Middle Ages," 1853.

[1] Dr Dunham says of his work : "It is well that it is sunk in oblivion.   No one reads it in Spain."

(10.) The Abbé *Rohrbacher.* "Histoire Universelle de l'Eglise Catholique." Paris, 1844. Vols. xi., xii., xiii

(11.) *Neander.* "General History of the Christian Religion and Church" (Bohn's Translation). Vol. v. pp. 218-233, 461-475 ; vol. vi. 119-132.

(12.) "Histoire d'Afrique et de l'Espagne sous la domination des Arabes," par *M. Cardonne.* 3 vols., 1765. A history based chiefly on Arab writers, but not very trustworthy, as Conde (Pref., p. 14) and Murphy (notes, passim) have shown.

(13.) *Dozy.* "Histoire des Mussulmans d'Espagne jusqu' à la conquête de l'Andalousie par les Almoravides, 711-1110." 4 vols., Leyden, 1861. An invaluable history of the time, being both lucid and thorough.

(14.) *E. A. Freeman.* "History and Conquests of the Saracens." Six lectures (ed. 1870). Spanish affairs are treated rather as a πάρεργον in Lecture v. An unprejudiced and accurate writer, with a strong bias, however, against chivalry (see Lecture v., p. 182).

(15.) *Ockley.* "History of the Saracen Empire" (Reprint in the Chandos Classics).

(16.) *Gibbon.* The parts relating to the Saracens are conveniently reprinted in the "Chandos Classics."

(17.) *Robertson's* "History of the Christian Church." Vol. iii.

(18.) *Milman's* "Latin Christianity." Bk. ix.

(19.) *Stanley.* "Lectures on the Eastern Church." Lect. viii.

(20.) *Hallam's* "Middle Ages." Vol. iii. (Chivalry).

(21.) *Geddes.* Expulsion of the Moriscoes, in his Miscellaneous Tracts. 1730.

Also Account of MSS. and Relics found at Granada in 1588 ; and View of Court of Inquisition in Portugal.

(22.) *Lecky's* "Rise and Influence of Rationalism in Europe." 2 vols.

(23.) *Buckle.* "History of Civilisation in England," chap. viii. "Spanish Intellect from Fifth to Nineteenth Centuries." Vol. ii. pp. 425-597.

(24.) *Carlyle.* "Hero Worship. The Hero as Prophet."

(25.) *C. M. Yonge.* "Christians and Moors in Spain." "Golden Treasury" Series. 1878. Obscure in method, and often inaccurate in facts. To give one instance only out of many—The authoress says (p. 29), that Ali, the son-in-law of the Prophet rebelled and died in battle. It is well known (Gibbon, vi. 274, 276) that he did neither.

(26.) *R. Bosworth Smith.* "Mohammed and Mohammed-anism." 1874. A brilliant, but essentially unfair book, Christianity being extolled in theory, but sneered at in practice. We are too forcibly reminded of "Brutus is an honourable man." His own accusation of others falls upon himself. P. 61, he says—"Most other writers have approached the subject only to prove a thesis. Mohammed was to be either a hero or an impostor: they have held a brief for the prosecution or the defence."

(27.) *S. Lane-Poole.* "The Moors in Spain." "Story of the Nations" Series. 1887. A clever and popular compilation from De Gayangos' translation of Al Makkari, Dozy, Southey's "Chronicle of the Cid," and Washington Irving's "Granada."

(28.) *Blunt.* "Dictionary of Sects, Heresies, and Schools of Thought." 1874. The articles on Mohammedanism, the Adoptionists, and others I have found very useful. There is, however, nothing said of the Priscillianists (of Spain), or the Druses.

(29.) *Hughes.* "Dictionary of Islam."

(30.) *The Koran.* Sale's edition.

(31.) *Encyclopaedia Metropolitana.* Vol. xi.

(32.) *Encyclopaedia Britannica.* Article on Averroes.

III. POETRY :—

(*a.*) *Lockhart's* "Spanish Ballads." 1823. Reprint, with Introduction, in the "Chandos Classics."

(*b.*) *Southey's* "Chronicle of the Cid." Reprinted, with Introduction, in the "Chandos Classics." A truly admirable translation.

(*c.*) *Southey's* "Roderic," with many interesting notes.

(*d.*) *Scott's* "Don Roderic."

IV. REFERRED TO :—

(*a.*) *Romey.* "Histoire D'Espagne." 1839. 4 vols.

(*b.*) *Reinaud.* "Invasion des Sarrasins." 1836.

(*c.*) *Mosheim.* "Institutes of Ecclesiastical History." Translated by Murdoch. 1845.

www.ingramcontent.com/pod-product-compliance
Lightning Source LLC
Chambersburg PA
CBHW022351020726
47500CB00002B/225